Growing Together in Christ

DENNIS FOUST
WESLEY SHOTWELL
DUANE BROOKS

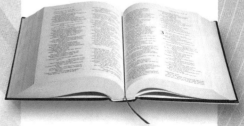

BAPTISTWAYPRESS®

Dallas, Texas

BAPTISTWAY PRESS® Management Team
Executive Director, Baptist General Convention of Texas: Randel Everett
Director, Missions, Evangelism, and Ministry Team: Wayne Shuffield
Ministry Team Leader: Phil Miller
Publisher, BAPTISTWAY PRESS®: Ross West

Cover and Interior Design and Production: Desktop Miracles, Inc.
Printing: Data Reproductions Corporation

First edition: June 2008
ISBN–13: 978–1–934731–07–9

How to Make the Best Use of This Issue

Whether you're the teacher or a student—

1. Start early in the week before your class meets.

2. Overview the study. Review the table of contents and read the study introduction. Try to see how each lesson relates to the overall study.

3. Use your Bible to read and consider prayerfully the Scripture passages for the lesson. (You'll see that each writer has chosen a favorite translation for the lessons in this issue. You're free to use the Bible translation you prefer and compare it with the translation chosen for that unit, of course.)

4. After reading all the Scripture passages in your Bible, then read the writer's comments. The comments are intended to be an aid to your study of the Bible.

5. Read the small articles—"sidebars"—in each lesson. They are intended to provide additional, enrichment information and inspiration and to encourage thought and application.

6. Try to answer for yourself the questions included in each lesson. They're intended to encourage further thought and application, and they can also be used in the class session itself.

If you're the teacher—

A. Do all of the things just mentioned, of course. As you begin the study with your class, be sure to find a way to help your class know the date on which each lesson will be studied. You might do this in one or more of the following ways:

- In the first session of the study, briefly overview the study by identifying with your class the date on which each lesson will be studied. Lead your class to write the date in the table of contents on page 7 and on the first page of each lesson.

- Make and post a chart that indicates the date on which each lesson will be studied.
- If all of your class has e-mail, send them an e-mail with the dates the lessons will be studied.
- Provide a bookmark with the lesson dates. You may want to include information about your church and then use the bookmark as a visitation tool, too.
- Develop a sticker with the lesson dates, and place it on the table of contents or on the back cover.

B. Get a copy of the *Teaching Guide*, a companion piece to this *Study Guide*. The *Teaching Guide* contains additional Bible comments plus two teaching plans. The teaching plans in the *Teaching Guide* are intended to provide practical, easy-to-use teaching suggestions that will work in your class.

C. After you've studied the Bible passage, the lesson comments, and other material, use the teaching suggestions in the *Teaching Guide* to help you develop your plan for leading your class in studying each lesson.

D. You may want to get the additional adult Bible study comments—*Adult Online Bible Commentary*—by Dr. Jim Denison, pastor of Park Cities Baptist Church, Dallas, Texas, that are available at www.baptistwaypress.org and can be downloaded free. An additional teaching plan plus teaching resource items are also available at www.baptistwaypress.org.

E. You also may want to get the enrichment teaching help that is provided on the internet by the *Baptist Standard* at www.baptiststandard.com. (Other class participants may find this information helpful, too.) Call 214–630–4571 to begin your subscription to the printed edition of the *Baptist Standard*.

F. Enjoy leading your class in discovering the meaning of the Scripture passages and in applying these passages to their lives.

Writers of This Study Guide

Dennis Foust, pastor of Shades Crest Baptist Church, Birmingham, Alabama, wrote unit one, lessons 1–3. Other churches Dr. Foust has served as pastor or associate pastor include Second-Ponce de Leon, Atlanta, Georgia; First, Chattanooga, Tennessee; and Manor, San Antonio, Texas. He received his master's and doctoral degrees from The Southern Baptist Theological Seminary, Louisville, Kentucky.

Wesley Shotwell wrote unit two, lessons 4–9. Dr. Shotwell is pastor of Ash Creek Baptist Church, Azle, Texas. He formerly was pastor of churches in Tennessee. He is a graduate of Baylor University (B.A.), Southwestern Baptist Theological Seminary (M.Div.), and Vanderbilt Divinity School (D.Min.).

Duane Brooks, the writer of unit three, lessons 10–14, is pastor of Tallowood Baptist Church, Houston, Texas. Dr. Brooks has been a member of the Executive Board and the Human Welfare Board of the Baptist General Convention of Texas and also of the Board of Regents of Baylor University.

Growing Together in Christ

DATE OF STUDY

UNIT ONE

Beginning the Journey

UNIT TWO

Growing in Christ

U N I T   T H R E E

Growing Together

This Study and Future Adult Studies

From the beginning of our BaptistWay® Adult Bible studies in March 2000, the studies we have offered have focused on Bible books or portions of Bible books. This approach has proven to be a most effective way of studying the Bible in order to understand its meaning and apply it to life. Many churches in various settings across the nation, and even some in other countries, have found the approach taken in our BaptistWay® materials to be helpful, and they return again and again to these materials as an aid to their study of the Bible.

Now, requests have come to provide an occasional Bible study that focuses on a biblical theme. This study, *Growing Together in Christ*, is at least partially in response to such requests. We hope you like it. We believe it provides a bit of variety. Even more important, it focuses on a biblical theme that is highly important, the theme of how we truly can grow together in Christ rather than being merely nominal Christians or people who are misguided about what being a Christian means. (See "Introducing Growing Together in Christ" for the introduction to the study.)

Further, in accord with sound principles of Bible study, we have taken care to keep the Scripture passages studied in the context of the Bible books in which they appear. As some wise Bible expositor said many years ago, *A text without a context is merely a pretext.* Although *Growing Together in Christ* is a study of a biblical theme, we believe the study sets the Scriptures in their biblical context rather than taking them out of context in order to try to promote (wrongly) a pet theme.

We will continue to emphasize studies of Bible books or portions of Bible books. Our present plan is to offer one study of a biblical theme each year.

Thank you for using our BaptistWay® materials. We work toward making each study one that will meet your needs. We value you, your Bible study class, and your church.

Here are some of the studies we are planning:

Ephesians, Philippians, Colossians: *Living with Faithfulness and Joy*	For use beginning September 2008
The Gospel of Matthew: *Hope in the Resurrected Christ*	For use beginning December 2008
Ezra, Nehemiah, Haggai, Malachi: *Restoring the Future*	For use beginning March 2009

Introducing

GROWING TOGETHER IN CHRIST

Growing Together in Christ is intended to help a church and its members focus on the opportunities and obligations of the Christian life and of members' life together. This study can be used in many ways to enhance the life of a church. Its prime use is in the church's ongoing Bible study program, but other possibilities include use as a study for a new church start and as a study for a new member class.

The study attempts to recognize the practical interplay that exists between what a church needs to be and do and what individual Christians need to be and do. Simply put and practically speaking, people tend to be most willing to help a church be and do what it needs to be and do as they are helped with their own individual concerns. Moreover, people are drawn more and more into the life of the church and the mission of Christ as they experience growth in their own lives.

Growing Together in Christ begins at the beginning. The first unit focuses on "Beginning the Journey." The first lesson in this unit calls the individual to respond to God's love. The second lesson recognizes the integral place in the salvation experience of being united with fellow believers in genuine church fellowship. These first two lessons thus combine the individual and church emphases. The third lesson emphasizes that becoming a Christian means committing oneself to follow Christ in every area of one's life and thus leads into the remainder of the study.

The second unit, "Growing in Christ," contains six lessons. The unit emphasizes six disciplines that prepare the way for the growth in the Christian life that God wants to give Christians. These six disciplines both enhance one's individual growth in Christ and also build up the church as individuals practice them.

The study moves next to consider some priorities a church should empha-size, as exemplified by the experience of the early church in Acts 2:42–47. This third unit, "Growing Together," consists of five lessons. An emphasis of this unit and of all of this study is that Christian growth is not simply about personal enhancement but about growth as part of a Christian com-munity, likely beginning with one's Bible study class but reaching toward one's fellow church members and the larger Christian community.

Beginning the Journey

Imagine you are about to begin a journey. The first step you take is extremely important. It will either align you more closely with your destination or move you farther from it.

Now, imagine you would like to help other people along on this same journey. You must decide whether you intend to be a travel agent or a travel guide. Travel agents perform helpful services. They interest you in the trip and provide some information about it but may never have journeyed down the roads you will travel. They give you your tickets, present to you a planner, and wish you well on your journey.

On the other hand, travel guides may say, *One time, when I was passing through this valley. . . .* Later, they may say something like, *I know it is challenging right now. However, just over this climb is a place to rest and be refreshed. These travel guides are able to say, I'm going to take you down some pathways with which I am familiar.*

The vast majority of people in the United States today find their lives characterized by the use of inventions and devices that help them get their needs met quickly and easily. Push buttons, switches, satellites, digital technology, remote controls, microwave ovens, and wireless access are common.

At the same time that we see our reliance on modern devices increases, we see an increased interest in hiking and wilderness exploration. People continue to seek opportunities to journey through new terrain—or even familiar terrain that is in the midst of change.

This study is about the journey of spiritual growth. There are no shortcuts or technologies that can make this journey pass more quickly or be accomplished more easily. The spiritual journey unfolds day by day as people struggle, give attention to the contour of the path, rest, tend to stings and cuts, climb, and find refreshment.

The first three lessons focus on the beginning of this spiritual journey. You will give attention to these lessons that call you to do these things: "Respond to God's Love"; "Get Together with Fellow Believers"; and "Decide to Live Christ's Way." In other words, these three sessions call you to consider the beginnings of spiritual transformation, a spiritual community of faith that enhances the journey, and the Lordship of Christ who has traveled the way before you. How you take these first steps will help you on your own journey and also help you be a better guide for others.[1]

UNIT ONE, BEGINNING THE JOURNEY

Lesson 1	Respond to God's Love	John 3:1–16
Lesson 2	Get Together with Fellow Believers	Acts 9:10–19; Romans 12:4–5; Hebrews 10:24–25
Lesson 3	Decide to Live Christ's Way	Mark 8:27–37; Romans 6:1–4

NOTES

1. Unless otherwise indicated, all Scripture quotations are from the New International Version.

FOCAL TEXT
John 3:1–16

BACKGROUND
John 3:1–21

MAIN IDEA
In love, God offers you eternal life if you will respond to Jesus, God's Son, whom God gave so that you might be saved.

QUESTIONS TO EXPLORE
How does God want you to respond to what God has done for you?

STUDY AIM
To respond to God's love by trusting in Jesus or to testify of how I have responded to God's love by trusting in Jesus

QUICK READ
Jesus' message of God's love is simple to understand for those people who sense the stirring breeze of God's Spirit in their lives and choose to respond positively to it.

LESSON ONE
Respond to God's Love

Sam was somewhat stooped by his ninety-one years. He was dearly loved and respected by everyone who knew him. Even his peers referred to him as "Mr. Sam." He had been asked to share his basic philosophy of life with a group of young adults. He sat before the young adults one Sunday morning, opened his well-used Bible to 1 John 4:7–10, and started to read in a slow, yet steady tone, "Dear friends, Let us love one another, for love comes from God. Everyone who loves has been born of God and knows God. Whoever does not love does not know God, because God is love. This is how God showed his love among us: He sent his one and only Son into the world that we might live through him. This is love: not that we loved God, but that he loved us and sent his Son as an atoning sacrifice for our sins."

Upon finishing his reading, Mr. Sam looked out at the group of young adults and said, "My life only has meaning because of the love of God. If you find anything at all in my life that is honorable or admirable, it is due to the love of God." He then said words that are still repeated by this group of young adults: "Before it is anything else, love is a choice. For you to love, you must choose to respond positively to God's love."

JOHN 3:1–16

[1]Now there was a man of the Pharisees named Nicodemus, a member of the Jewish ruling council. [2]He came to Jesus at night and said, "Rabbi, we know you are a teacher who has come from God. For no one could perform the miraculous signs you are doing if God were not with him."

[3]In reply Jesus declared, "I tell you the truth, no one can see the kingdom of God unless he is born again."

[4]"How can a man be born when he is old?" Nicodemus asked. "Surely he cannot enter a second time into his mother's womb to be born!"

[5]Jesus answered, "I tell you the truth, no one can enter the kingdom of God unless he is born of water and the Spirit. [6]Flesh gives birth to flesh, but the Spirit gives birth to spirit. [7]You should not be surprised at my saying, 'You must be born again.' [8]The wind blows wherever it pleases. You hear its sound, but you cannot tell

where it comes from or where it is going. So it is with everyone born of the Spirit."

⁹"How can this be?" Nicodemus asked.

¹⁰"You are Israel's teacher," said Jesus, "and do you not understand these things? ¹¹I tell you the truth, we speak of what we know, and we testify to what we have seen, but still you people do not accept our testimony. ¹²I have spoken to you of earthly things and you do not believe; how then will you believe if I speak of heavenly things? ¹³No one has ever gone into heaven except the one who came from heaven—the Son of Man. ¹⁴Just as Moses lifted up the snake in the desert, so the Son of Man must be lifted up, ¹⁵that everyone who believes in him may have eternal life.

¹⁶"For God so loved the world that he gave his one and only Son, that whoever believes in him shall not perish but have eternal life.

The Love of God

Society suggests, *Love is a feeling you feel when you feel a feeling you have never felt before.* Yet, a stirring within the human spirit desires for love to be more than an emotion that is dependent on momentary whims. People desire for love to be more than temporarily tangible. In every human dwells a deep desire for love to be spiritually substantive and transcendent. There is a desire to find love at the core of life, not at its periphery. People long for love to be invigorating in the most important aspects of their lives. Humans desire for love to be a steady stream of living water that renews and nourishes and never changes in its essence.

"God is love," wrote John. Of all the characteristics God could have chosen to be the central ingredient in God's own being, God chose love. This must be the answer to the question Job asked in the midst of his suffering, "What is man that you make so much of him, that you give him so much attention?" (Job 7:17).

Jesus Christ calls his followers to the depths of faith in the midst of a shallow world. While the world wants to point merely to flowers and birds and speak of the love of God, Christ's church points to the most despicable sins and impulses of humanity and says, *God's love is bigger than that.* In a world that wants to focus on entertainment and excitement, Christ calls people to focus on the eternal truths revealed in the love of God.

God is love. As height, depth, and breadth are used to help us understand the dimensions of the tangible, so grace, mercy, forgiveness, redemption, reconciliation, joy, peace, and hope are used to explain the dimensions of the spiritual. "God is love," exclaims John. God is expressed through a variety of dimensions; yet, each reflects love.

Responding to God's Love Is a Possibility for Everyone and Anyone (3:1–2)

Have you heard the good news? No matter what you have done—or not done; no matter who you are—or are not; you can experience the love of God. You cannot experience the love of God just because you decide you want to do so. However, you can respond to the stirring of the Spirit within you that creates a thirst to know God in a personal relationship. You can respond to God's love no matter who or what you have been.

John 3 introduces us to a story of one person's encounter with Jesus as an *after-dark story*. In some stories, Jesus went to people. In other stories, Jesus stopped by people along the path. In this story, Nicodemus "came to Jesus" (John 3:2).

To some extent Nicodemus represents the old understanding of religion, the pre-Christ perspective. It is significant that Nicodemus approached Jesus under the cover of darkness. Nicodemus was a member of the Jewish ruling council, the Sanhedrin. He was an extremely influential person in Jerusalem. Had he approached Jesus in the middle of the day, among the people, this experience and the conversation could have been entirely different.

We are not told whether this conversation between Nicodemus and Jesus was pre-arranged or serendipitous. We are not even told why Nicodemus approached Jesus. What we are told is that Jesus saw into Nicodemus's life and discerned that the Pharisee was looking for spiritual light, although he approached Jesus in the darkness.

Clearly Nicodemus and other influential religious leaders were listening to and noticing the ministry of Jesus. Possibly Nicodemus was reporting conclusions reached among the religious leaders of Jerusalem when he said, "we know you are a teacher who has come from God. For no one could perform the miraculous signs you are doing if God were not with him" (3:2).

Most likely, the religious leaders thought they had figured out God's ways. In their minds, God worked through insightful teachers and miracle workers. This was part of Israel's history. They could point to numerous teachers, prophets, and miraculous moments through which God had shaped their history. No doubt, Nicodemus sensed that Jesus reflected this same line of divine revelation. It had not occurred to Nicodemus, though, that a whole new spiritual experience was being revealed in the person of Jesus. There was a stirring of the Spirit in Nicodemus. A new wind was blowing, and it caused a fresh breeze in Nicodemus. He "came to Jesus" (3:2).

Responding to God's Love Requires a New Birth (3:3–8)

Early in Nicodemus's conversation with Jesus, he heard a new idea and a new phrase, *born again*. Do you remember the first time you heard the

FREEDOM—AND RESPONSIBILITY— TO EXPRESS FAITH

One tradition of Christian practice that emerged during the Protestant Reformation was a movement called Anabaptism. Anabaptists taught there must be a conscious decision to commit one's life to Jesus as Lord of one's life. They rejected infant baptism and practiced believer's baptism. They were called *Ana-Baptists*, meaning *to baptize again* (*ana* means *again*). Later, the earliest Baptists, around 1611, embraced the principle of soul competency, the idea that a person's faith is based on a conscious commitment to Christ as Lord rather than a mental affirmation of creedal or doctrinal uniformity.

Baptists have historically embraced the idea that every human is created in the image of God, has the freedom of choosing to express faith in Jesus Christ or not, and thus also is accountable to God for his or her decision. Baptists have been careful to embrace the freedom of the person to respond to God's love and have emphasized the need for a faith commitment through a spiritual new birth.

phrase? Has it been part of your spiritual language ever since you can remember? In the southern United States, this phrase is common among Baptists. However, if you did not grow up Baptist, or if your roots are not in the southern states, you may have first learned the phrase when you dated a Baptist during high school. Or, you may have been introduced to the phrase when it was used to describe narrow-minded students during your college years. Has the term *born again* always had a good connotation in your mind? Would you describe yourself to your neighbors and co-workers as a *born-again* Christian?

When Jimmy Carter was elected president of the United States in 1976, he identified himself as a born-again Christian. Prior to Jimmy Carter, the White House press had never expressed so much interest in the phrase, *born again*. Now we hear the phrase more often in the media.

This phrase, *born again*, is a metaphor we use to describe the spiritual new birth that occurs when a person experiences God through the love revealed in Jesus Christ. This response to God's love transforms human lives and transforms the world. The Greek word often translated *born again* can also be translated *born from above*. To respond to the love of God is to be born through the Spirit of God into a personal relationship with God, as revealed in Christ.

Nicodemus, true to form for a man who carefully followed each detail of the law, focused on the earthly implications and limitations communicated by the idea of being born again. Yet, Jesus was pointing Nicodemus to consider the spiritual perspective of a new birth. Isn't that just like Jesus to push a person toward a perspective higher than the earthly viewpoint?

CONTRASTS IN JOHN 3:1–21

Note the contrasts in John 3:1–21:
- Light with darkness (Night)
- Above with below
- Spirit with flesh
- Heavenly with earthly
- Life with death
- Saved with condemned
- Love with hate

For a person to experience the love and power of the kingdom of God, a new birth from above is necessary. On the one hand, Nicodemus was correct. It is impossible for a person to be reborn as a physical person. Yet, Jesus called Nicodemus to a higher realm of understanding. It is possible for a person to be reborn as a spiritual person. Only God, the eternal Holy Spirit, can give a new birth to a person, as the person believes in Christ.

Responding to God's Love Is Both Confusing and Simple (3:9–16)

Nicodemus would have understood Jesus' words about a new birth if Jesus had described a list of external behaviors or expectations. If, in order to be a follower of Jesus, a person needed to fulfill certain obligations, as in the case of a Gentile who chose to become a Jew, Nicodemus would have made a note, nodded his head, and returned to the Sanhedrin with a report. Yet, while Jesus' revelation of the love of God was simple to understand, Nicodemus was confused by his message.

Nicodemus belonged to the group of Jewish leaders who observed every aspect of the Torah, that is, the Jewish law. This group eventually both led and redefined Judaism after the destruction of Jerusalem in the year A.D. 70. Yet, here Jesus was almost mocking Nicodemus's lack of spiritual understanding. You could paraphrase Jesus,

> You are one of the brightest minds in all Israel and you cannot understand the simple spiritual truths I am saying to you. Nicodemus, if you cannot understand my explanation of this new birth when I use earthly metaphorical language, how in the world do you expect to understand me if I use spiritual language?

For centuries, children, youth, and adults in almost every culture around the world have responded to the love of God revealed in Jesus Christ. Is it because Jesus' message is simple? Yes, Jesus' message of God's love is quite simple to understand for those people who sense the stirring breeze of God's Spirit within their spirit and choose to respond positively. In fact, God's love, revealed in Jesus, is taught in John 3:16 and is memorized by people in thousands of languages: "For God so loved the world that he gave his one and only Son, that whoever believes in him shall not perish but have eternal life."

Implications and Actions

Jesus also taught, "A new command I give you: Love one another. As I have loved you, so you must love one another. By this all men will know that you are my disciples, if you love one another" (John 13:34–35). The love of God must affect the way we live in relationship with one another. Once we have been *born from above*, our lives must reflect God's love to others. We respond to God's love by being *born from above*. And, we respond to God's love as we ourselves love one another.

QUESTIONS

1. What experience have you had of responding to God's love and being *born again* or being *born from above*? How would you describe it to another person?

2. What are some reasons it can be so difficult for some people to understand this idea of a spiritual new birth?

3. Jesus said, "I tell you the truth, no one can see the kingdom of God unless he is born again [*born from above*]" (3:3). How do you feel about these words? Do they compel you to share your faith with others? Do they inspire you to pay closer attention to the implications of your witness or your character in relationship to others?

4. Is it possible to sense evidence in a person's life as to whether the person has experienced a spiritual new birth? If not, why not? If so, what evidence do you identify?

5. How does a person's life change once he or she responds positively to God's love?

FOCAL TEXT

Acts 9:10–19;
Romans 12:4–5;
Hebrews 10:24–25

BACKGROUND

Acts 9:1–30; Romans 12:4–8;
Hebrews 10:24–25

MAIN IDEA

Giving encouragement to and receiving encouragement from fellow believers by joining in fellowship with them in the church is an essential part of the Christian life.

QUESTION TO EXPLORE

How important is the church in the Christian life?

STUDY AIM

To recognize the importance to my Christian life of joining in deepening fellowship with fellow believers

QUICK READ

After you respond positively to God's love, you will find Christ's church to be a helpful network of relationships that will help you grow as a follower of Jesus.

LESSON TWO

Get Together with Fellow Believers

Janice called her longtime neighbor. After a quick hello, Janice said, "Trudy, my life has changed. I responded to God's love last weekend while visiting my sister. My life is different, and I need to talk to someone who can understand."

Trudy almost shouted into the phone, "Oh, Janice, this is wonderful news! Do you know I have been praying for you to begin a relationship with Jesus? I guess I have been praying for you since we moved next door to you twelve years ago."

"Trudy," Janice interrupted, "I need you to help me know how to follow Jesus. My parents were Christians, and they took us girls to church until they divorced when I was twelve. But that was years ago. I am not sure where to start. You are the only Christian friend I have here in San Antonio. My sister asked me if I had any Christian friends, and you were the only person who came to my mind. Will you help me learn how to grow as a Christian?"

Trudy smiled into the phone, "Sure I will, Janice. I am blessed you have asked me to help you. This is a privilege and a gift of God's grace you are giving to me. In fact, I know exactly where we can begin. Please ride to church with us this Sunday. But, first, I will come over to your house in the next couple of days so we can study through the Bible study lesson together. I cannot wait to introduce you to my other friends at church and them to you."

You may be a person with many close friends, the kind of friends you would trust with your checkbook. Or, you may feel at times as though you have nobody in your life who really cares for you. Even if you do not have trustworthy people in your family or friendship circles, once you respond to God's love you will find other people who truly care for you in a local church.

ACTS 9:10–19

10 In Damascus there was a disciple named Ananias. The Lord called to him in a vision, "Ananias!"

"Yes, Lord," he answered.

11 The Lord told him, "Go to the house of Judas on Straight Street and ask for a man from Tarsus named Saul, for he is praying. 12 In a vision he has seen a man named Ananias come and place his hands on him to restore his sight."

13"Lord," Ananias answered, "I have heard many reports about this man and all the harm he has done to your saints in Jerusalem. 14And he has come here with authority from the chief priests to arrest all who call on your name."

15But the Lord said to Ananias, "Go! This man is my chosen instrument to carry my name before the Gentiles and their kings and before the people of Israel. 16I will show him how much he must suffer for my name."

17Then Ananias went to the house and entered it. Placing his hands on Saul, he said, "Brother Saul, the Lord—Jesus, who appeared to you on the road as you were coming here—has sent me so that you may see again and be filled with the Holy Spirit." 18Immediately, something like scales fell from Saul's eyes, and he could see again. He got up and was baptized, and 19after taking some food, he regained his strength.

ROMANS 12:4–5

4Just as each of us has one body with many members, and these members do not all have the same function, 5so in Christ we who are many form one body, and each member belongs to all the others.

HEBREWS 10:24–25

24And let us consider how we may spur one another on toward love and good deeds. 25Let us not give up meeting together, as some are in the habit of doing, but let us encourage one another—and all the more as you see the Day approaching.

No Believer Is an Island (Acts 9:10–19)

Ananias was a follower of Jesus who lived in Damascus. Perhaps he had professed faith in Jesus as the Messiah through the preaching of some Christians from Jerusalem. He had also heard about a Jewish man named Saul (Paul) of Tarsus who had persecuted the Christians in Jerusalem and who had traveled to Damascus to do the same. The

Lord told Ananias that Saul was God's chosen instrument to preach to Gentiles and kings. The Lord instructed Ananias to find the recently-blinded Saul and restore his sight. As you can imagine, Ananias did not want to go. However, the Lord insisted, and Ananias obeyed.

As you follow Jesus, you will find that your obedience guides you to do things for other people you would not naturally do. We find Ananias ministering to a person whom he would have refused to care for had he been influenced only by the news reports. Yet Ananias knew the voice of the Lord in his life and obeyed it.

Paul had been *born from above* while on his way to Damascus. He understood the Lord had come into his life in a new way. Paul, who was traveling around persecuting Christ's followers, had now become a Christian. In his blindness, he was led into Damascus by his travel companions. Paul was baptized as a new believer, a new disciple. None of his spiritual experiences occurred in a vacuum. Paul began to experience a spirituality that can only be lived in relationship with other believers.

After you experienced your spiritual new birth, you may have found yourself wanting and needing to be with other Christian people. This is as it should be. You need to find a group of people who together are following Christ. Once you responded to God's love, you found yourself desiring to have a relationship with other people who have experienced the spiritual birth.

Another point to ponder in these verses is that Christ's church consists of people who may be quite different from one another. Sometimes these differences require believers to move past their prejudice and fear. This was the case for Ananias. He had to overcome his concerns about Paul to minister to him.

As we meet other disciples, we must move beyond our prejudice and fear. We find that new vision results from one life touching another. Blindness passes away and the waters of baptism introduce new potential as your life touches and is touched by the faith of others.

Saul of Tarsus became known as the Apostle Paul. He was God's primary messenger to Gentiles. He preached the good news of God's love revealed in Christ to the cultural, intellectual, political, and economic centers of the Roman Empire. Before beginning his work, Paul spent "several days" with the other Christians in Damascus (Acts 9:19). No doubt, he always kept a special place in his heart for these first disciples of Jesus who welcomed him into their lives. No believer is an island. We need one another.

The stories and roles of Paul and Ananias in Christ's church were quite different. Ananias never became a household name. Yet, he expressed faithfulness to the Lord's message at a significant time in Paul's life. Their roles in the history of Christ's church were different, but nonetheless connected. Each one was essential.

The Body of Christ: Unity Through Diversity (Romans 12:4–5)

The human body consists of many and diverse parts with varied functions and roles. In like manner the body of Christ finds and expresses unity through diversity. Just as the human body would be diminished in capacity and strength if it sought to operate without unity through diversity, so the body of Christ is diminished when it does not recognize its diversity.

Paul wrote to the believers in Rome about their need to focus on unity by belonging to one another. In his letters to the Christians in Rome, Corinth, Ephesus, and Colossae, Paul used the word *body* more than thirty times to illustrate the unity of Christ's church and how it was to function. Paul experienced this kind of unity at his new birth in Christ through Ananias accepting him.

While a local community of believers is an expression of the unity people find in Christ, a local church also includes other aspects of a living body. Each member of Christ's church is a human being. Therefore, be aware that a local body of Christ will also include pain, conflict, and brokenness, for these exist in the lives of its members. Some people are more inclined to follow what the world teaches than what is taught by Christ. Some are more familiar with competition than with allowing time and space for diverse individuals to grow and mature. Some find it impossible to care for others because they require intense care themselves. Some are much better at independence than interdependence. Some have a low threshold of tolerance for diversity, and so they manipulate people into pathways of uniformity or into rigid lines of authority.

Paul offered the analogy of the human body as a living reminder to the members of Christ's church for all generations. We need one another. The eye cannot say to the leg, *I no longer need you*. Neither can the

CHECK YOURSELF

For centuries, Baptist congregations have embraced a ministry called Sunday School or Bible Study. This ministry of the local
church has contributed much to the relational life of Christians. In
fact, this is the way most Baptist church members meet together
for encouragement, prayer, Bible study, and deepening friendships.
Yet, some people seem to make it a habit of not meeting together.
Their names are on the church rolls, but they seem to believe they
do not need to meet with other Christians.

Sometimes it is good to look in the mirror and ask hard questions.

- Do outsiders find our group to be friendly and welcoming?
  What evidence do we have?

- Do people come looking for a community of believers who
  take seriously the challenges of maturing in Christ but find a
  group of people who are so intimidated by the teachings of
  Christ that they give them as little attention as possible?

- Do we truly seek to follow Christ and encourage one another
  in doing so?

parent of a preschooler say to an older adult, *you are no longer needed in
this body.* The energy and the wisdom of diverse age groups are needed.
Each one belongs to one another.

You need to belong to and participate in a local body of believers, even
with all of its idiosyncrasies—and even its hypocrisies. You have been
born again, born from above. The body of Christ is the body to which
you belong.

Christ's Scattered and Gathered Church (Hebrews 10:24–25)

Belonging to the body of Christ should always encourage you toward
becoming a more mature follower of Jesus. As you get together with
other believers, good questions to ask include, *Am I seeking to grow
deeper in my relationship with Jesus Christ? Am I maturing as a witness
of the character of Christ in the world? If every member of this local church*

was the kind of disciple I am, would the church be stronger or weaker? Nobody should belong to a local church in order to strive for mediocrity although that is a danger faced by many churches.

The Letter to the Hebrews speaks to several issues that were relevant in the first century and are also relevant in the twenty-first century. One of these issues is the need for Christians to be involved in the lives of one another. In Hebrews 10:24–25, the need for Christians to be involved in one another's lives is addressed in two ways.

First, Christians need to consider how to encourage one another to express the love of God through good deeds. Christ's church does not exist just to meet the needs of its members. The mission or purpose of Christ's church also includes sharing God's love with people outside the church.

By staying in touch with other members of Christ's church, you can encourage one another to pursue the teachings of Jesus. Today's technologies, such as cell phones, e-mail, and text messaging, enable Christ's church to be in touch instantaneously and almost without geographic boundaries. You can remind one another of God's promises. You can help one another see the need for consistency in commitment. You can pray and encourage those who sin and fail. You can support those who are struggling with moral, financial, relational, vocational, and ethical challenges. You can share your ideas for ministry and hear the ideas of others. You can celebrate victories and share burdens.

Second, Christians need to meet together. The phrase, *high tech–high touch* is certainly relevant for Christ's church today. Just as a note from a spouse or a phone call from a child is appreciated, people value your e-mails and text messages. But nothing takes the place of that hug from your spouse or child. Being in their presence is essential for you to thrive. The same holds true for the members of the body of Christ.

Christ's church lives as the scattered church in the world for most of every week. You may not have seen the other members of your class or group since last Sunday or longer. You and your fellow church members generally live through most of the week as the scattered church. However, you need to meet together regularly with them. You need to be Christ's gathered church.

The focus of the gathered church should be on equipping and encouraging the members of Christ's body to be healthier witnesses of the character of Christ during the times they are scattered. You get to choose

YOU CAN HELP

You can contribute to the health and spiritual renewal of your congregation by

- expressing a more consistent compassion for others
- exploring a deeper journey into prayer
- asking church leaders how you can pray for them and with them about their desire to mature as followers of Jesus

whether you will be a positive or a negative contributor to significant Christian community. You are one or the other.

Implications and Applications

You have been *born from above*. You have responded positively to God's love. You now belong to the body of Christ. As other Christian's lives touch yours, your blindness subsides and you begin to clarify what it means to follow Jesus as your Lord. Most days, you are scattered in the world to live out the character of Christ and his vision of ministry in the world. However, you also need to be getting together with fellow believers.

You need to be involved in Christ's gathered church in order to be involved more faithfully in God's mission while you are Christ's scattered church. Your ministry in the world will be more fulfilling to you if you gather with other believers. Just as a marriage fractures if the spouses spend little or no time together and just as parent-child relationships are nurtured in healthy ways by time together and time separate from one another, so the lives of fellow believers are fractured or healed by time together and time apart.

QUESTIONS

1. Who have been the people like Ananias in your life, people who have helped you receive your sight along the journey of faith?

2. In what ways does your congregation intentionally embrace diversity? Can you name some ways your church could be more open to diversity and more supportive of unity? Are there ways in which your church has fallen victim to those who believe uniformity—everybody being alike—to be the basis of fellowship?

3. Are there people or people groups to whom you or your congregation fail to minister because of prejudice or fear? If so, who and why?

4. What can you and your class/group do to include more people?

5. What does it mean to you that you *belong* to the congregation? How does *belonging* encourage you in your *becoming* more like Christ? How does *belonging* shape your life?

FOCAL TEXTS
Mark 8:27–37; Romans 6:1–4

BACKGROUND
Mark 8:27–37; Romans 6:1–4

MAIN IDEA
Christians are to commit
themselves to following Christ
in all the areas of their lives.

QUESTION TO EXPLORE
What does being a
Christian mean to you?

STUDY AIM
To commit or recommit
myself to following Christ
in all the areas of my life

QUICK READ
After you have responded to
God's love and have begun
getting together with fellow
believers, God's Holy Spirit
will shape every dimension of
your life under the authority
of Christ's Lordship.

LESSON THREE
Decide to Live Christ's Way

William stood before the congregation on a Wednesday evening to share his spiritual autobiography. His pastor had asked William and seven other church members to tell their own life stories during a two-month emphasis called "Living the Story."

William began his spiritual autobiography with these words, "I first responded to God's love at the age of nineteen. I knew about Jesus. Our family attended worship two or three Sundays a year. We always went to worship when my Grandmother Southerland came for her annual visit from Arkansas. However, I did not grow up in the church."

"During my sophomore year at the university, I asked a girl out on a date. She said the only way she would date me was if I accompanied her to Sunday School and worship on Sunday mornings. I asked her if she meant every Sunday and she said 'yes.'"

"Three months later, I asked our Sunday School teacher to meet me for lunch one day. That afternoon, I responded to the invitation of Jesus, who said, 'Follow me.' On that day, February 9, 1974, I chose to allow the Lord to set the desires for my life. My ambitions and goals were transformed. You have watched my life for many years now. You know I am imperfect in every way. Yet, because of my relationship with Jesus, my life has a character, a mission, and a fulfillment that I could never have known otherwise."

William then looked at a middle-aged woman sitting at a table to his left, his wife of thirty-two years, and said, "Thank you again, Josephine, for setting that requirement of Sunday School and worship attendance for our dating relationship."

After telling about other experiences of his life, William concluded, "I remember what the pastor said to me on the day of my baptism. After he brought me up out of the water, he placed his hands atop my head and said, 'William, your life is no longer your own. You have given your life to Jesus Christ. He is your Lord and you are now a minister in the work of his kingdom.' Every day, I hear those words echoing in my memory: 'Your life is no longer your own. Your life is no longer your own.'"

MARK 8:27–37

27 Jesus and his disciples went on to the villages around Caesarea Philippi. On the way he asked them, "Who do people say I am?"

28 They replied, "Some say John the Baptist; others say Elijah; and still others, one of the prophets."

29 "But what about you?" he asked. "Who do you say I am?"

Peter answered, "You are the Christ."

30 Jesus warned them not to tell anyone about him.

31 He then began to teach them that the Son of Man must suffer many things and be rejected by the elders, chief priests and teachers of the law, and that he must be killed and after three days rise again. 32 He spoke plainly about this, and Peter took him aside and began to rebuke him.

33 But when Jesus turned and looked at his disciples, he rebuked Peter. "Get behind me, Satan!" he said. "You do not have in mind the things of God, but the things of men."

34 Then he called the crowd to him along with his disciples and said: "If anyone would come after me, he must deny himself and take up his cross and follow me. 35 For whoever wants to save his life will lose it, but whoever loses his life for me and for the gospel will save it. 36 What good is it for a man to gain the whole world, yet forfeit his soul? 37 Or what can a man give in exchange for his soul?

ROMANS 6:1–4

1 What shall we say, then? Shall we go on sinning so that grace may increase? 2 By no means! We died to sin; how can we live in it any longer? 3 Or don't you know that all of us who were baptized into Christ Jesus were baptized into his death? 4 We were therefore buried with him through baptism into death in order that, just as Christ was raised from the dead through the glory of the Father, we too may live a new life.

Who Is Jesus to You? (Mark 8:27–30)

Since you are reading this lesson, you likely have responded to God's love and belong to a Sunday School class or Bible study group. Possibly, some of your best friends are in this class. You are sharing life with these people. They know you are a Christian. However, another question is worth consideration: Do these people know who Jesus is to you?

The Gospel of Mark includes this story of Jesus and the disciples that occurred in the region near Caesarea Philippi. The disciples were followers of Jesus. Still, Jesus asked them who people thought he was. The disciples replied that people were saying he was John the Baptist or Elijah or one of the prophets. Then Jesus asked his followers, "Who do you say that I am?"

Where Jesus and the disciples were when he asked this question is significant. Caesarea Philippi was a city at the foot of Mount Hermon and was named for Tiberias Caesar and Herod Philip. The city was dedicated to the Roman Empire, and nearby could be found a temple dedicated to Augustus. Near this city dedicated to a temporary, made-with-human-hands-kingdom, Jesus began to direct the attention of his followers to a new level of commitment, a higher vision, and an eternal kingdom.

The question Jesus posed to the disciples was, *What about you?* "You are the Christ," was Peter's response. "Christ" is the English rendering for the Greek word, *Christos*, which means, *the anointed one*. "Christ" is the equivalent of the Old Testament word that is often translated into English as *Messiah*. Prophets, priests, or kings were anointed when they officially entered their offices. By giving to Jesus the title *the Christ*, Jesus was anointed as prophet, priest, and king.

Jesus' followers acknowledged him to be the fulfillment of the Old Testament prophecies. They believed him to be God's Anointed One, the one whom all Jews believed would restore the dynasty of David and begin the eternal reign of God over God's chosen people. Of course, Jesus did fulfill those prophecies. Jesus' followers were not wrong. They failed to realize, though, that the kingdom proclaimed by Christ operated in the lives of individuals who professed Jesus as their Lord. God reigns but not everyone realized that then, or now. God's rule will become obvious to everyone when Jesus returns.

Mark's Gospel begins, "The beginning of the gospel about Jesus Christ, the Son of God." In the Mark 8 passage, as Jesus ended his ministry in

BAPTISTS AND THE LORDSHIP OF CHRIST

From the beginning of Baptist history, the concept of the Lordship of Christ has been embraced. The Lordship of Christ is the foundation for Baptists when they emphasize the competency of the individual before God and when they stress autonomy in their congregational polity.

In order to express freedom of conscience or volition, a person must be able to relate directly with God, through Jesus Christ as Lord. If a believer is expected to relate to God under the authority of a creed or any statement enforcing doctrinal uniformity, a layer has been placed between the believer and the believer's freedom in directly and obediently responding to the Lordship of Christ.

In like manner, the autonomy of a congregation is essential to the members expressing obedience to the Lordship of Christ in the life of the faith community. According to principles historically embraced by Baptists, no association, convention, fellowship, or alliance can have authority over the congregation as it lives under the Lordship of Jesus Christ. For Baptist individuals and congregations, Jesus is Lord. Jesus has authority over our lives, and we will not give greater authority to any other person, organized body, or doctrinal statement.

Galilee and turned his face toward Jerusalem, his identity as the Christ was affirmed once again. Later, in Mark 14, Mark recounted Jesus' appearance before the Sanhedrin on the morning after his arrest. In Mark 14:61, the high priest asked Jesus, "Are you the Christ, the Son of the Blessed One?" Jesus responded, "I am."

These three passages (1:1; 8:29; 14:61) frame Mark's Gospel. Mark pointed to Jesus as the Christ, the *Messiah*, from the beginning of his Gospel. This proclamation was repeated by his followers as Jesus set his face toward Jerusalem. Too, this message was confirmed by Jesus as he entered his suffering and sacrificial death.

As a follower of Jesus, you have confessed your belief that Jesus is the Christ. God's Anointed One came proclaiming to humanity the kingdom of God that is realized by those who humbly allow him to be Lord in their lives. You may want to consider what professing Jesus as Lord of your life means for you. Following Jesus does not lead down a primrose path. Jesus' first followers had to learn this reality. All of his followers must learn it.

The Christ Who Rebukes (Mark 8:31–33)

Jesus followed Peter's statement by explaining to his disciples that he was going to suffer many things, be rejected by the religious authorities, be killed, and rise again after three days. He talked plainly about the details of the coming days.

Simon Peter, the same disciple who said, "You are the Christ," took Jesus aside and spoke to Jesus as though he was Jesus' equal. Simon Peter rebuked Jesus for talking as he had done. Mark did not tell us exactly what Peter said. However, one can imagine that Peter might have said things such as: *Jesus, you have got to stop talking like this. Sometimes you scare me. You are Messiah! You are God's Anointed One! Nothing bad can happen to you. When you start talking about things like this, the people turn away from you. They want to hear good news, not gruesome talk about suffering and death.*

APPLYING THIS LESSON'S KEY THEMES

As you consider the key themes of this lesson, you might apply its teachings by

- writing out your spiritual autobiography
- writing out your statement of who Jesus is to you
- identifying experiences when you have sensed Jesus' rebuke
- naming ways you are carrying your cross of discipleship today
- recording the meaning of your baptism as a symbol of your walk with Christ
- listing the aspects of your life that challenge Christ's Lordship
- listing ten hymns that help you focus on the Lordship of Christ
- listing ten Scripture passages that help you focus on the Lordship of Christ

Whatever Peter said, Jesus evidently changed his body posture before he responded. In Mark's telling of the story, we read, "But when Jesus turned and looked at his disciples." Can you imagine the facial expression of Jesus that the disciples might have seen? Do you think they had ever seen this expression on Jesus' face before this time?

The same disciple who had confessed Jesus to be the Christ is now called "Satan" by Jesus. Then Jesus rebuked Peter with words no follower of Jesus ever wants to hear: "You do not have in mind the things of God, but the things of men" (Mark 8:33).

Are you familiar with the Christ who rebukes? Have you ever had in mind the methods or perspectives of human design rather than the methods and perspectives of divine design? Have you ever sensed in your spirit the rebuke of Christ's Spirit, convicting you of a sinful view of a situation?

The Way of the Cross Leads Home (Mark 8:34–37)

Jesus' pathway included a cross. Therefore, if you are going to follow Jesus on his pathway, it too must include a cross.

The only way to follow Jesus, the Christ, is to deny your selfish desires, take up your cross, and follow him. If you choose to believe Jesus is the Christ and still pursue your self-centered desires, you will lose the life of discipleship. However, if you choose to lose your self-centered life because you are committed to Christ, you will experience the abundant life of discipleship. Believing Jesus to be the Christ is not enough to be Jesus' disciple. Even the demons believe he is the Christ. You must follow Jesus by the way of the cross.

If you were to gain the whole world, what would you have without Jesus? Are you going to give your life to something like fortune, notoriety, or pleasure? Are these worth your soul? What exactly is worth the value of your discipleship?

The good news is that if you are following Jesus, he has already gone ahead of you. Whatever you must relinquish as his follower, he has already relinquished. If you must leave certain loyalties or allegiances or possessions or interests behind in order to carry your cross of discipleship, Jesus understands. In order to experience the victorious resurrection life as a follower of Jesus Christ, you must walk the pathway of the cross.

Your Baptism and the Lordship of Christ (Romans 6:1–4)

As we approach the end of this lesson and the unit of study on "Beginning the Journey," considering whether Jesus Christ is truly your Lord is important. *Lordship* is the term used to acknowledge who or what has authority in your life. You acknowledge the Lordship of Christ in your life when you profess, "Jesus is the Christ." Too, you acknowledge the Lordship of Christ in your life when you accept his rebuke in your spirit. Further, you daily acknowledge the Lordship of Christ in your life as you deny your self-centered desires, take up your cross of discipleship, and begin to learn and live as a follower of Jesus wherever he leads you.

In writing to the early Christians in Rome, Paul pointed out that grace always abounds more than sin. This raised the question, "What shall we say then? Shall we go on sinning so that grace may increase?" His answer was, "By no means!" The basis of his answer is the Lordship of Christ in the life of the believer.

Paul proposed that someone who has died to sin cannot go on sinning. Paul taught that you share in the death of Jesus Christ through your baptism. By his death, sin is overcome and reconciliation with God is now your experience. Through your response to God's love and through your commitment to Jesus Christ, you have died to the power of sin. Your baptism symbolized your dying to the power of sin and to your pursuit of selfishness.

In addition, just as you share in Christ's death, you also share in Christ's resurrection. Just as Christ's death was a victory over sin, his resurrection was a victory over death. Just as your baptism symbolizes your death to pursuing a life of sin, your baptism also symbolizes your resurrection to a new life—a life that pursues the character of Jesus, the Christ.

You proclaim in your baptism, *Jesus is my Lord*. This truth was introduced with the story about William who heard echoes of his pastor's words at his baptism, "Your life is not your own!" "Your life is not your own!"

Implications and Actions

If you listed all the things you love, how many pages of paper would you need to complete your list? Is there anyone or anything on your list that you love more than Jesus Christ? Sometimes people are willing to follow Jesus by giving up possessions, accolades, prestige, position, friends, and even family. But they are unwilling to sacrifice themselves.

Other people are willing to give up themselves but are unwilling to place their vocation, finances, marriage, or children under the Lordship of Christ. They have experienced the grace of God to the extent that their sins are forgiven and their life's purpose is envisioned. They believe they are capable of restructuring their lives around the Lordship of Jesus Christ until they come upon that one thing or that one person they are unwilling to love less than Jesus. If there is anything or anyone in your life that you love more than Jesus, then that item or idea or cause or institution or person is your lord.

QUESTIONS

1. Do you agree or disagree with the idea that upon becoming a disciple of Jesus Christ, your life is not your own? Why or why not?

2. Who do people today say Jesus is? Who do you say Jesus is? How do you proclaim Jesus as the Christ in your daily life?

3. Would you be willing to share with your group a time when you knew Jesus was rebuking you?

4. Is it possible for a Christian or a congregation to emphasize either Jesus as Savior or Jesus as Lord more than the other? Explain.

5. Do you think baptism is emphasized more as a symbol of death to sin or as a resurrection to new life? What are some ways your church could enhance its observance of baptism?

Growing in Christ

The Christian life is more than walking down the aisle and being baptized. That may be the beginning of the Christian life, but it is only the beginning. The Christian life is one of spiritual discipline that allows God to continue to work in us so we can grow to spiritual maturity.

Unit two identifies and describes six spiritual disciplines that help us grow into mature Christians. These six lessons explore the growing process of the Christian. Jesus calls us to be disciples, that is, followers or learners. We cannot be disciples without discipline. These six lessons do not exhaust all the practices of the Christian life, but they get us off to a good start.

A disciple is first of all a learner, and the first lesson explores the discipline of learning. Other lessons focus on the disciplines of serving, giving, worship, Christlike relationships, and right living. These disciplines can help all Christians, whether they are new believers or have been Christians for many years. The disciple's life is an ever growing one that does not reach complete maturity until we are with the Lord in heaven.[1]

UNIT TWO, GROWING IN CHRIST

Lesson 4	The Discipline of Learning	Matthew 11:28–30; John 14:23–26; 1 Corinthians 3:1–3; Hebrews 5:11–14
Lesson 5	The Discipline of Serving	John 13:3–17
Lesson 6	The Discipline of Giving	2 Corinthians 8:1–9; 9:6–8
Lesson 7	The Discipline of Worship	Mark 1:35–36; Luke 4:16; 11:1–4; Philippians 4:6
Lesson 8	The Discipline of Christlike Relationships	Matthew 18:15–17, 21–35; 2 Corinthians 2:5–11
Lesson 9	The Discipline of Right Living	Colossians 3:1–14

NOTES

1. Unless otherwise indicated, all Scripture quotations are from the New International Version.

FOCAL TEXT
Matthew 11:28–30; John
14:23–26; 1 Corinthians
3:1–3; Hebrews 5:11–14

BACKGROUND
Matthew 11:25–30; John
14:23–26; 1 Corinthians
3:1–4; Hebrews 5:11–14

MAIN IDEA
To be a disciple of Jesus is to
learn continually from Jesus.

QUESTION TO EXPLORE
What steps are you taking
to seek continually to
learn from Jesus?

STUDY AIM
To decide on ways I will seek
continually to learn from Jesus

QUICK READ
Growing disciples of Jesus
Christ are learning continually
about what being a true
follower of Christ means.
Spiritual maturity goes
beyond the basics of the
faith by accepting Jesus'
invitation to keep learning
from him for a lifetime.

LESSON FOUR
The Discipline of Learning

Every morning when I get out of bed I go into my sons' bedrooms and wake them up. After the hustle and bustle of getting ready, we pile into the car, and away we go to school. When I drop them off, I tell them to have a good day. The last thing I say to them every morning is, "Learn something today!" I don't know how seriously they take my advice. Every evening I ask them if they learned anything today. Invariably they say no. It is somewhat discouraging.

But I know they have learned something because I can see the progress they have made through the years. When they began school they could not read or write or add or subtract. Now they can do all of those things—and more! They can read complicated books; they can do algebra and geometry; they can write essays; and they can do science projects. It has taken a while, but they are no longer learning the ABCs. They are becoming more and more intellectually mature.

Being a disciple of Jesus means being a learner. Whereas a person can become a Christian in a single moment in time, the spiritual maturity of Christians is developed over a lifetime as they learn more and more. Jesus invites us into his school so that we will get beyond the basics of the faith and become spiritually mature.

MATTHEW 11:28–30

28"Come to me, all you who are weary and burdened, and I will give you rest. 29Take my yoke upon you and learn from me, for I am gentle and humble in heart, and you will find rest for your souls. 30For my yoke is easy and my burden is light."

JOHN 14:23–26

23Jesus replied, "If anyone loves me, he will obey my teaching. My Father will love him, and we will come to him and make our home with him. 24He who does not love me will not obey my teaching. These words you hear are not my own; they belong to the Father who sent me.

25"All this I have spoken while still with you. 26But the Counselor, the Holy Spirit, whom the Father will send in my name, will teach you all things and will remind you of everything I have said to you. [27]Peace I leave with you; my peace I give you. I do not give to you as the world gives. Do not let your hearts be troubled and do not be afraid.

1 CORINTHIANS 3:1–3

[1]Brothers, I could not address you as spiritual but as worldly— mere infants in Christ. [2]I gave you milk, not solid food, for you were not yet ready for it. Indeed, you are still not ready. [3]You are still worldly. For since there is jealousy and quarreling among you, are you not worldly? Are you not acting like mere men?

HEBREWS 5:11–14

[11]We have much to say about this, but it is hard to explain because you are slow to learn. [12]In fact, though by this time you ought to be teachers, you need someone to teach you the elementary truths of God's word all over again. You need milk, not solid food! [13]Anyone who lives on milk, being still an infant, is not acquainted with the teaching about righteousness. [14]But solid food is for the mature, who by constant use have trained themselves to distinguish good from evil.

Enrolling in School with Jesus (Matthew 11:25–30)

Jesus does not save us and then forget us. He takes people who have come to him and invites them to a lifetime of learning.

The background text depicts Jesus praising God because God had revealed the deep mysteries of the kingdom of God to "little children" who were ripe for learning. Their willingness to learn contrasts to those who think themselves to be wise and who think that they already know it all. The first step to learning in the school of Jesus is to have the attitude of a child who knows that there is much to learn. God has revealed things to Jesus that he wishes to reveal to us, but we must be ready to learn.

Jesus invited people who were weary and burdened to come to him that he might give them rest. We must be careful to keep this statement in context. It does not promise that following Jesus will be easy. Many people, like the martyrs, have discovered that the life of a disciple is not always easy.

The context becomes clear when we consider Jesus' invitation to his disciples to take his yoke upon them. The first picture that comes to mind when we think of a yoke is a wooden collar on the necks of oxen so that they could be harnessed to a wagon or a plow. The rabbis referred to the law when they spoke of a yoke. By the time Matthew's audience read these words, the 613 commandments identified in the law had been elaborated on by traditions, rules, and regulations. A person had to have special training as a lawyer to keep up with what was right and wrong. The law had been designed to help people live good lives, but it had evolved into such a burden that it had become a source of bondage.

In contrast, Jesus says when you are his student the way is not burdensome. His invitation is open to all who labor under the burden of the law. The rest Jesus offers is not an escape from work or the stress of life. Rest comes from the security of knowing the forgiveness of sin and the acceptance by God by faith, not from the law.

Jesus' students can breathe a sigh of relief. In Jesus' school, learning is not the achievement of the wise and intelligent. Learning is not solely

THE PROBLEM IN CORINTH

The Corinthian church existed in the midst of a pagan culture that was known for its immorality and self-indulgence. The people were accustomed to an egocentric philosophy that encouraged self-promotion and pride. This attitude seems to have carried over into the church because the church was divided into factions. Each faction was promoting itself at the expense of others in the church.

This spirit of division was antithetical to the gospel. The gospel insisted that believers love one another and that the church be united in love. But the Corinthians evidently had not learned this basic truth of Christian life. They were demonstrating spiritual immaturity by tearing one another down in order to promote their own agenda. They had much to learn about being a disciple of Jesus!

about propositions and facts. Learning is about growing in relationship with God and with others.

Meeting the Teacher (John 14:23–26)

In the hours just before Jesus was crucified, he gave a farewell address to his disciples. He knew he would no longer be with them in bodily form. How then would they learn from him? The question was relevant not only to the first disciples but also to every follower of Jesus today.

Obviously Jesus is not here in bodily form. As Jesus' followers, we need a teacher for all time if we are going to obey him. Jesus said our teacher is the Holy Spirit.

Jesus made it very clear that disciples would demonstrate their love for him by obeying his teaching. Obedience to his teaching is not slavish legalism based on fear. Obedience to Jesus is based on love and is modeled by the servant attitude that he demonstrated.

Obedience based on love results in God's Spirit dwelling in the believer. Christians need not fear abandonment because God has set up a permanent dwelling place with us.

God lives with us as the Holy Spirit. The Holy Spirit is a gift from God who teaches us how to obey Jesus' words. The Spirit is not a new and improved version of God. The Spirit does not teach us new truths that go beyond what Jesus taught. He does, however, deepen our understanding of what Jesus taught. The Spirit confirms Jesus' teaching and reminds us of how to obey him while we are living in this world.

Failing to Make the Grade (1 Corinthians 3:1–3)

The Corinthians had much to learn about following Jesus! They had come into the kingdom from a pagan culture and needed to learn what it meant to live like a Christian in a pagan world. They were like newborn babies who needed to be fed with their mother's milk so that they would grow and mature to a point of being able to digest heartier meals.

By the time Paul wrote to the Corinthian church, some of them had been Christians for several years. You would have thought by then they were mature enough to move on to the deeper, meatier truths of the

TOOLS FOR LEARNING FROM JESUS

Which of these tools for learning from Jesus are you using?

- Openness to the prompting of the Holy Spirit
- Bible study by oneself and in small groups
- Prayer
- Practicing biblical stewardship
- Regular corporate worship
- A willingness to learn

faith. But even after these years had passed, they were no more mature than they were when they first met Christ. They had made so little progress that Paul was frustrated, like a teacher whose students could not promote to the next grade.

The tragedy of failing to learn from Jesus is prolonged immaturity. Spiritual learning is more than intellectual knowledge. It is growth in relationship with God and with others.

I have two children. I remember very well when we brought each of them home from the hospital and put them in the baby bed we had set up in our house. They were small and defenseless and did not know anything about this world or how to relate to it. So my wife and I taught them in various ways. When the time came we sent them to school, and they have learned even more about living in society with others. In short, they are now maturing and will soon be grown men. How tragic it would be if they stayed little babies lying in a baby bed all of their lives. How sad it would be if they never learned right from wrong or how to relate to society. Yet, millions of believers never grow beyond spiritual birth. They never grow into spiritual adults and never learn how to relate to God or to others in church. How sad!

Paul knew the Corinthians had failed to mature because they demonstrated their immaturity by continuing to act as they did when they first became believers. They were worldly. Their worldliness was evident because there was still jealousy and quarrelling among them. They were fighting about who was the most spiritual among them. They never recognized the irony that their fighting revealed that they were spiritually immature. Their self-interests stunted their growth.

Sometimes mature believers ought to stand against injustice and fight for what is right. But the fight must always be in God's interest and not our own. Fighting that is motivated by self-interest often results in name-calling, slander, division, and broken relationships. These acts surely demonstrate spiritual immaturity. Such a person is not ready to move on to the next grade and must be retained for remedial instruction.

Stuck in Kindergarten (Hebrews 5:11–14)

The readers of Hebrews found themselves in a situation similar to the Corinthians. They had not learned very quickly and needed to be retained so they could learn the basics of their faith.

The writer of the book wanted to explain some things to them but was finding it difficult to put into words what they should know because they had not grown enough to grasp what he was trying to say. This should not have been the case. By this time these people had been believers long enough that they should have been instructing others about the faith. Instead, they were content to stay in immaturity.

They were still in spiritual kindergarten. The writer says they still needed someone to "teach you the elementary truths of God's word all over again." The word translated "elementary truths" means learning the ABCs or the rudimentary principles of the faith. They should have been teachers by now, but they did not even know the basic foundation.

Have you known people who ought to have matured in their faith but still lacked a basic foundation? They may have been Christians for a long time, but they have no interest in Bible study or stewardship or church life. They relate to others in a worldly manner. They have no idea how to share their faith with another person. They do not pray. They seem satisfied with staying in spiritual kindergarten learning the ABCs and have no interest in promoting to higher grades.

The writer of Hebrews used the same metaphor Paul used in 1 Corinthians 3:2. People who fail to promote out of spiritual kindergarten must be fed milk because they are still spiritual babies. They cannot bear the rigors of spiritual adulthood. If they are not handled carefully, their immaturity may cause disunity in the church or spiritual failure.

These people cannot be trusted to make wise and spiritual decisions because they are not even acquainted with righteousness.

Heartier spiritual food and responsibility can and should be fed to those who have demonstrated maturity. But be careful not to feed meat to those who are unable to digest it.

Occasionally I hear suggestions that we should put an individual who seldom attends church on a committee or even make the person a deacon. The reasoning is that if we would give the person some responsibility the person would attend more. In practice, this strategy for church participation does not work. But the greatest danger is theological. We must not feed meat to those who have demonstrated they cannot digest it yet.

Implications and Actions

Learning from Jesus is a spiritual discipline. Jesus taught his disciples when he was on earth and continues to teach his followers today through the Holy Spirit. It is vitally important that we continue to be learners. If we fail to continue learning, we will not be able to be all God wants us to be.

Learning from Jesus is more than intellectual learning of facts and propositions and more than knowing doctrine. Facts and doctrine are important, but we may know people who are well-schooled in theology and Bible facts but are spiritually immature. Spiritual maturity is about one's relationship with God and with other people. Most of the time Bible knowledge and doctrine help give us understanding that can lead to maturity, but maturity is more than intellectual knowledge.

Have you learned anything lately? You may feel like my children who go to school every day but never think they are learning anything. But look back at your spiritual life over the past year, or five years, or ten years. Can you see progress?

QUESTIONS

1. Think back to an earlier time in your Christian life. In what ways are you different now? How can you learn more from Jesus?

2. Imagine you are on a committee that will choose new deacons for your church. What are the characteristics of the kind of person you would choose to be a deacon? How do those qualities identify that the person you have chosen is a learner?

3. Imagine that the Christian life is like attending school. What grade are you in right now? Are you promoting to the next grade from time to time or have you been stuck in the same grade for years? What criteria did you use to determine whether or not you promoted?

4. What opportunities does your church offer to help you learn from Jesus? How often do you take advantage of them? In what ways can you take better advantage of them?

5. Name a new Christian whom you could help mature as a follower of Jesus. What are some things you can do to help this new Christian learn and become more mature?

FOCAL TEXT
John 13:3–17

BACKGROUND
John 13:1–17; 1 John 3:16–18

MAIN IDEA
Serving others is a characteristic of genuine Christian living.

QUESTION TO EXPLORE
Is serving other people just an option for a Christian?

STUDY AIM
To decide on ways I will express the Christian attitude of service

QUICK READ
Jesus demonstrated what genuine Christian discipleship looks like by stooping down to do the lowliest task of service. Followers of Jesus are called to follow his example and serve other people regardless of personal cost.

LESSON FIVE
The Discipline of Serving

The power and influence of serving others cannot be overestimated. Max Depree, CEO of a company and an author of books on leadership, wrote in *Leadership Jazz:*

> I arrived at a local tennis club just after a group of high school students had vacated the locker room. Like chickens, they had not bothered to pick up after themselves. Without thinking too much about it, I gathered up all their towels and put them in a hamper. A friend of mine quietly watched me do this and then asked me a question that I've pondered many times over the years. "Do you pick up towels because you're the president of a company, or are you the president because you pick up towels?"[1]

The night before Jesus was to be raised up on the cross, he reached down and picked up a towel. Jesus picked up the towel because he was the Savior who understood that he was a suffering-servant kind of Savior. His taking up the towel demonstrated to his disciples what it meant to be a servant of others. He stooped down to serve them by washing their feet. Jesus, the King of kings, performed the task reserved for the lowest slave of society. This demonstration of service and humble sacrifice foreshadowed the sacrifice that he would make the next day. The crucifixion was the ultimate gift of service that demonstrated the full extent of Jesus' love for even the lowliest of the low.

JOHN 13:3–17

[3] Jesus knew that the Father had put all things under his power, and that he had come from God and was returning to God; [4] so he got up from the meal, took off his outer clothing, and wrapped a towel around his waist. [5] After that, he poured water into a basin and began to wash his disciples' feet, drying them with the towel that was wrapped around him.

[6] He came to Simon Peter, who said to him, "Lord, are you going to wash my feet?"

[7] Jesus replied, "You do not realize now what I am doing, but later you will understand."

8"No," said Peter, "you shall never wash my feet."

Jesus answered, "Unless I wash you, you have no part with me."

9"Then, Lord," Simon Peter replied, "not just my feet but my hands and my head as well!"

10Jesus answered, "A person who has had a bath needs only to wash his feet; his whole body is clean. And you are clean, though not every one of you." 11For he knew who was going to betray him, and that was why he said not every one was clean.

12When he had finished washing their feet, he put on his clothes and returned to his place. "Do you understand what I have done for you?" he asked them. 13"You call me 'Teacher' and 'Lord,' and rightly so, for that is what I am. 14Now that I, your Lord and Teacher, have washed your feet, you also should wash one another's feet. 15I have set you an example that you should do as I have done for you. 16I tell you the truth, no servant is greater than his master, nor is a messenger greater than the one who sent him. 17Now that you know these things, you will be blessed if you do them.

Serving in the Dark (John 13:1–5)

A dark side to the story of Jesus washing the disciples' feet makes what happens even more remarkable. It was the night of the Passover Feast. Jesus was observing the Passover with his disciples. Passover was a particularly poignant event since the Passover lamb was slain for the sins of the people. John reminded us of the presence of a sinner in the room. He noted that the devil had already entered into Judas Iscariot, the one who would betray Jesus, the Lamb of God. Although we cannot know the motives of Judas, they likely were prompted by selfish and worldly ambition.

John also reminded us that grace was present in the room. Jesus found himself among his dearest friends. Even among them, he was surrounded by deceit, betrayal, doubt, and jealousy. They were arguing about who was the greatest among them. In the midst of this darkness, Jesus was about to show them the light of love. The example Jesus would give them was but a foretaste of the servant love he would show the next day.

The synoptic Gospels—Matthew, Mark, and Luke—center the events of this night on the Last Supper. They do not mention the incident about washing feet while John did not mention the Last Supper. John emphasized the service and sacrifice of Jesus as the Lamb of God, which Jesus demonstrated by humbling himself to serve others in the lowly task of foot-washing.

Foot-washing was a filthy task and was reserved for the lowliest slave of a household. Many slaves were exempt from having to perform this nasty task because washing the mud and muck off another person's feet was so demeaning. The job was assigned to the slave of the slaves. Yet Jesus, who had authority over everyone, lowered himself to selfless service for the sake of others.

The story contrasts the attitudes of Judas and Jesus. The servant, Judas, took it upon himself to become the master; Jesus, the Master, voluntarily humbled himself to become the servant. Jesus became the servant of slaves. Judas, who had no authority, sought to use worldly power to get what he wanted for himself; Jesus, who had ultimate authority, gave himself in service for others. Judas sought honor; Jesus shamed himself in order to honor God. Unfortunately, I suspect that many of us are more like Judas and less like Jesus than we would like to admit.

Serving When Misunderstood (John 13:6–11)

Jesus washed his disciples' feet, presumably even Judas's. John did not record anyone objecting to Jesus' actions until Peter piped up. Even though no one but Peter said anything, he may have been voicing the sentiment of everyone in the room. It must have been an uncomfortable moment for all of them, so uncomfortable it left them speechless.

If you can count on anyone to speak up, you can count on Peter. Peter asked, "Lord, are you going to wash my feet?" (13:6). His words were more of an objection than a question. We might better understand it as *You are not going to wash my feet, are you?*

This act of service made no sense to Peter. He could sense the paradoxical nature of this moment, but he could not understand its meaning. In fact, Peter seemed offended because the voluntary shame of Jesus shamed Peter. Peter knew that if anyone should be washing feet, it should be the disciples washing Jesus' feet. Yet, as Jesus usually did, he turned the world upside down by doing things that made no sense in this world.

Jesus assured Peter that even though he did not understand these strange actions now, soon he would understand them. But Peter could see only the ways of this world. He could not see or understand the ways of the kingdom until later.

Peter was operating out of a culture that valued honor and reviled shame. Honor meant that one had authority in the community and other people served that person. But if you served another person you were shamed because you had to admit that the person was better than you. Jesus' act of humble service had the opposite effect in Peter's life. Peter must have been shamed that the person with authority was serving him. He could not understand what Jesus was doing because he was still operating in the ways of this world.

Peter completely missed the point and strongly objected. In the Greek, he used the emphatic double negative in his denial: *You will not, never wash my feet.* In English a double negative is poor grammar, but in Greek it is emphatic. Peter was objecting in the most stringent terms.

BAPTISM, THE LORD'S SUPPER, AND FOOT-WASHING

Most Baptists recognize two ordinances of the church: baptism and the Lord's Supper. Some Baptist and Mennonite traditions have practiced a third ordinance: foot-washing.

Foot-washing used to be practiced more among Baptists in the United States than it is now. This tradition probably came from the Anabaptists in Europe and continued when believers came to the New World. Today, however, the practice is limited to a few denominations. It may be more widely practiced in dramatic form in association with Maundy Thursday worship services.

Although Jesus told us to do as he did, he was not necessarily telling us to practice literal foot-washing as a ritual of the church. He was demonstrating the meaning of humble service toward others. However, it may be helpful from time to time to witness or participate in a literal foot-washing service as a dramatic and symbolic reminder of Jesus' command to love one another in humble, sacrificial service. What do you think?

Peter meant well by his objection. He did not want Jesus to be shamed. But clearly he did not understand the eternal meaning of the moment because he was still thinking in the temporary context of his culture.

Jesus gave Peter a choice. Either you get your feet washed or you don't have me at all. You must take me as a servant or you can't take me. Jesus was giving Peter the same choice he gives to all of us. We accept Jesus as an humble, suffering servant who gave his life for us, or we do not accept him at all.

Peter then responded in his typical over-the-top way. *Don't stop with my feet, then. Wash all of me!* It is almost a comic response. Peter went from one extreme to the other in a matter of seconds. Again Peter missed the point. This conversation was not about taking a bath.

Peter had understood Jesus' act as a simple physical washing of the feet, but Jesus understood it as a new way of thinking about authority. Jesus' example of washing feet became a lesson about his kingdom. This was not about getting their feet clean. It was about a new way to live and think. Peter and the other disciples could not understand this until after they had witnessed the crucifixion and resurrection.

Serving One Another (John 13:12–17)

Next came the moment of instruction. After experiencing this remarkable act of service, the disciples needed some explanation for this event that had turned everything on its head.

Jesus asked, "Do you understand what I have done for you?" I am not convinced that they did. What had happened was more than Jesus physically washing their feet. Jesus did not ask them whether they *knew* what he had done. He asked them whether they *understood* what he had done. In other words, did they understand what this remarkable act meant?

Jesus admitted that they had rightly understood him as their superior. He was their Teacher. He was their Lord. What they had not understood was how Jesus defined the role of a superior in God's kingdom. In God's kingdom, the bigger you are the lower you stoop to serve others.

Jesus' action gave the disciples a graphic example of what it meant to be great in the kingdom. Judas did not understand; he sought greatness by pursuing his own agenda. Peter did not understand; he sought greatness in the context of his cultural values. But Jesus knew that greatness

---

IDEAS FOR SERVING

- Organize a class project that will serve someone with whom you may not ordinarily have contact.
- Participate in a project that meets human need beyond your community and state.
- Visit a nursing home. Hold the hands of the people there who may not receive another human touch today.
- Volunteer at your local food bank.

---

comes only by serving others, even if it means being a servant of slaves. The act of washing their feet gave a model for all disciples of Jesus to follow.

Jesus' example does not mean that we should go around washing people's feet all the time. Modern transportation and better footwear have rendered literal foot-washing obsolete. But it does mean that if we are going to be mature followers of Jesus we must be humble servants to others. An unwillingness to serve others is a stark indication that we have not learned much about Christian discipleship.

Serving others may cost more than just giving up a Saturday afternoon to help a neighbor mow his yard. There have been times when serving others has cost Christians their lives. We should not be surprised at this. Jesus gave his life for us as the ultimate example of humble service. As followers of Jesus, how can we do any less?

Later John wrote about humble service in a letter. In 1 John 3:16–18, John reminded his readers that since Jesus laid his life down for us Christians we must be willing to lay down our lives for others. This may or may not take the form of literal loss of life in this world, but it always costs us something. John gave the example of sharing our material possessions with a person in need. Love must be more than words; love works.

Jesus ended this lesson with a truth that many Christian servants have discovered. Serving others is a great blessing. Jesus promised that God's blessing is on believers who live out their faith in serving others. And remember, in God's kingdom the lower you stoop the bigger you are.

Implications and Actions

Serving people is a spiritual discipline that is a strong indicator of spiritual maturity. If we are going to be like Jesus, we cannot serve our own agenda or be driven by personal ambition. We must transcend cultural barriers that keep us from serving some people when our culture tells us that some people are better than others.

Another way to think about this is to ask how we define success. In the case of Judas, success was defined by whatever self-centered motive he had. Somehow he must have believed that betraying Jesus would advance his agenda. Peter defined success in terms of the shame and honor conventions of his culture. For Peter, success was receiving honor from the community while failure was being shamed by the community. In both cases success was defined in terms of this world. Things have not changed that much, have they?

Jesus saw things from another world. He saw things from the standpoint of the kingdom. For Jesus, success had nothing to do with a personal agenda or with living up to the expectations of society. It had only to do with living up to God's expectations and agenda.

Which world motivates your actions? If you are motivated by this world, your actions will serve your own needs and desires. But if you are motivated by God's world, you will serve God by serving others, even if you must be a servant of slaves.

QUESTIONS

1. Who would you identify as the lowliest class of people in our society? What needs do they have that you could meet? What are some tasks you could perform for them that you might consider beneath you? Choose one and set a time to do the task.

2. Think of a person in your church who is proficient in the discipline of serving. What are the qualities about that person you would consider emulating?

3. What are some personal or cultural barriers that prevent believers from serving others?

4. Have you ever had the feeling that you are too good to serve a certain person? Have you ever prevented someone from serving you because you thought they were too good to stoop down to serve you?

NOTES

1. Max DePree, *Leadership Jazz: Weaving Voice with Touch* (New York: Doubleday, 1992), 218–219.

FOCAL TEXT
2 Corinthians 8:1–9; 9:6–8

BACKGROUND
2 Corinthians 8—9

MAIN IDEA
Giving ourselves to the Lord
leads us to give ourselves and
our material possessions to
minister to other people's
needs and advance the
work of the gospel.

QUESTION TO EXPLORE
What does being a Christian
have to do with giving?

STUDY AIM
To identify how truly giving
myself to the Lord affects
my giving of time, energy,
and material possessions
and evaluate my life in
light of these truths

QUICK READ
Paul encouraged the
Corinthians to give to the
Jerusalem relief fund by telling
them about the sacrificial gift
the Macedonians had already
given and by reminding them
that God blesses his people
when they are generous givers.

LESSON SIX
The Discipline of Giving

A pastor once appealed for his church to support a worthy cause. A woman member of the church handed him a check for $50 and asked whether that was satisfactory. The pastor replied, "If it represents you."

She thought for a moment or two and asked the pastor to give her back the check. She returned a couple of days later with a check for $5,000 and asked the same question, "Is my gift satisfactory?"

The pastor replied, "If it represents you."

The woman again took back her check and returned later with one for $50,000. As she handed it to the pastor, she said, "After earnest, prayerful thought, I have come to the conclusion that this gift does represent me, and I am happy to give it."

Paul encouraged the Corinthians to give generously and gratefully. He offered them an opportunity to support a worthy cause. He was taking up a collection of funds from the churches in Europe and Asia that would be sent back to the poor Christians in Jerusalem who were suffering economic hardship as a result of famine and persecution. He had asked the Corinthians previously to give (1 Corinthians 16:1–4), and they had pledged that they would. Evidently the offering had been delayed, perhaps because of their strained relationship with Paul. Now Paul was writing them to encourage them to fulfill their previous pledge.

The collection of these funds was more than an effort to meet physical needs. This gift of grace served to link the churches in a common cause. The collection gave Gentile believers an opportunity to participate in ministry toward Jewish Christians. Paul must have hoped this generous gift of grace would help Jewish believers to accept the theologically suspect Gentiles into the fellowship of the church. The gift would prove that the grace of the gospel had extended to all people.

Giving to the collection was more than raising money. It was about building believers into mature disciples of Christ.

2 CORINTHIANS 8:1–9

¹And now, brothers, we want you to know about the grace that God has given the Macedonian churches. ²Out of the most severe trial, their overflowing joy and their extreme poverty welled up in rich generosity. ³For I testify that they gave as much as they were able, and even beyond their ability. Entirely on their own, ⁴they

urgently pleaded with us for the privilege of sharing in this service to the saints. [5]And they did not do as we expected, but they gave themselves first to the Lord and then to us in keeping with God's will. [6]So we urged Titus, since he had earlier made a beginning, to bring also to completion this act of grace on your part. [7]But just as you excel in everything—in faith, in speech, in knowledge, in complete earnestness and in your love for us—see that you also excel in this grace of giving.

[8]I am not commanding you, but I want to test the sincerity of your love by comparing it with the earnestness of others. [9]For you know the grace of our Lord Jesus Christ, that though he was rich, yet for your sakes he became poor, so that you through his poverty might become rich.

2 CORINTHIANS 9:6–8

[6]Remember this: Whoever sows sparingly will also reap sparingly, and whoever sows generously will also reap generously. [7]Each man should give what he has decided in his heart to give, not reluctantly or under compulsion, for God loves a cheerful giver. [8]And God is able to make all grace abound to you, so that in all things at all times, having all that you need, you will abound in every good work.

Encouragement from the Example of Other Believers (8:1–7)

Paul encouraged the Corinthians to give by telling them about the generous gifts the churches in Macedonia had given. These churches were composed of the believers in Philippi, Berea, and Thessalonica. These were not wealthy churches. In fact, just the opposite was true. Paul said that the Macedonians were in severe poverty and trial. The word for "severe" means *down to the depths* or *at rock bottom*. But even at rock bottom they were overflowing with Christian joy and bubbling up with generosity.

Christian giving is not just for the wealthy but is a discipline for all believers. Paul linked monetary giving to the grace of God. Since we have received the grace of God, our giving becomes a channel of God's grace to others.

The Macedonians gave more than what might have been expected. They did not give out of their surplus because they had no surplus. They gave out of their deficit. Some people give out of their surplus. If they have some money left over at the end of the month, they give that to the Lord. However, most of the time they buy stuff or have to pay a debt on stuff they already bought and don't have any surplus. But the Macedonians gave out of their scarcity and trusted God to take care of them.

Paul did not compel the Macedonians to give. He did not try to force money out of them. Their giving was self-initiated and self-motivated because they understood God's grace. They not only gave when asked; they even begged for the privilege of giving. They had a concern for people beyond themselves. They looked beyond their own needs and desires to care for the needs of people they had never seen. It was quite a contrast with the Corinthians. The Corinthians had been embroiled in controversy about their personal preferences and could not see outside themselves. This is often the case when there is disruption in the church. We become inwardly focused. But Paul wanted the Corinthians to see the example of the Macedonians who looked outward.

The reason the Macedonians were able to look outside themselves to the needs of others is found in 2 Corinthians 8:5. Paul said, "they gave

CHEERFUL GIVING

The Greek word translated "cheerful" is the word from which we get our words *hilarious* and *exhilaration*. God blesses those who give with hilarity. Sometimes people give grudgingly and then wonder why they do not reap a harvest of joy. If we give with grief over lost dollars, God's blessing will likely elude us. We are demonstrating that we don't really trust God to take care of us.

Cheerful, hilarious, exhilarating giving is a demonstration that we trust God to give us what we need. God's grace frees us from grief and guilt so we can overflow in giving to others.

themselves first to the Lord and then to us." After they had given themselves to God, they were able to give their money because they had come to realize that their money belonged to God anyway. Christian giving is not really about giving our money; it is about giving ourselves. When we have given ourselves, we can focus on others rather than ourselves.

The Corinthians, despite all their problems, were a gifted congregation. They were gifted in faith, in speech, in knowledge, and even in love. But they lacked something. They were incomplete in giving. They had pledged to give to the fund but had not fulfilled that pledge. Paul sent Titus to them to encourage them to be complete in the discipline of giving. After all, they could not experience true Christian maturity until they gave themselves and their money.

Paul pleaded with them to excel in the grace of giving in the same way that they had excelled in other disciplines of Christian life. He wanted them to experience the blessing of being a channel of God's grace to others.

Encouragement from the Example of Christ (8:8–9)

Paul made it clear that he was not forcing them to give. He was not even trying to use his apostolic authority to command them to give. He recognized that coerced giving does not result in love but in resentment.

Giving is at the very heart of the gospel. The ultimate example of giving was Jesus Christ, who gave up his own life for humanity. Jesus was rich but made himself poor by coming to this world and giving himself for others. The gospel is all about giving.

A man in a church I used to serve got mad every time I preached about Christian giving. He would quit coming for three or four weeks after one of those sermons. He told me, "You ought to stop preaching about giving and stick to preaching the gospel." It was rather clear to me he didn't understand the gospel. After all, the heart of the gospel says that *God so loved the world that he gave.*

I heard about one man who came to church and heard a sermon about Christian giving. After the service he stormed up to the preacher and spat out, "As far as I can see, this Christian business is just one continuous give, give, give!" The preacher simply replied, "That is the best definition of Christianity I have ever heard."

Jesus gave himself for us. Jesus set the example for us. Giving is not just a part of the gospel; it is the heart of the gospel.

Encouragement from an Example in Nature (9:6–8)

Paul quoted a proverb from the agricultural world to remind the Corinthians that giving to the Lord's work is not throwing money away but is an investment with a promise of blessing. Paul pictured a farmer who goes out into the field to plant seed. The farmer thinks to himself, *If I plant all these seeds I won't have any seeds left. I think I will just plant a few seeds and keep the others safe in the barn.* He plants three seeds. When harvest time comes he climbs on his tractor and drives to the field to reap his crop. It doesn't take very long. He has only three plants to harvest, and he receives only a few pennies when he sells his crop. His neighbor, on the other hand, risked all his seeds. His harvest was huge. What is true in the natural world is also true in the spiritual world.

The word "generously" literally means *with blessing* (8:6). In other words, if we sow a blessing we will harvest a blessing. Now don't get me wrong. I am not saying that if you give a lot of money, God is going to give you a lot of money. The preachers of health and wealth, *seed-faith* theologies are misleading people. They feed off the greed of people who think they can get rich by giving to those organizations. But what we receive when we give is worth 100 times more than money. When we invest in the kingdom, we are a part of helping to change the lives of people. Giving to the Lord is not throwing money away. It is investing in the growth of the kingdom of God, and God can multiply that money to change lives.

Christian giving is more than just throwing money into the plate. Christian giving is more about motive than money. Paul told the Corinthians to give as each of them had decided in their hearts. He instructed them not to give out of a sense of duty or coercion. Giving must be cheerful. Cheerful giving is when you know that your gift is in accordance with God's will. Joy comes from wanting to give to God, not from having to give.

The telephone rang in the pastor's office. The voice on the other end of the line said, "This is the Internal Revenue Service calling. We need your help."

IDENTIFYING MINISTRIES THAT MATTER

Make a list of the ministries that your church does because people give. Think about the lives that are changed because of these ministries. Study your church budget, and identify how the things in it make a difference in God's kingdom.

The pastor's stomach began to tighten up as he meekly answered, "I'll do the best I can."

"Do you know Bruce Wayne Parker?" the agent asked. The pastor confirmed that Bruce was indeed a member of his church.

"Did he donate $100,000 dollars to your building fund?"

A smile came across the pastor's face as he answered, "If he hasn't yet, he will!" I have a feeling that Bruce was about to give because he had to, not because he wanted to.

You will find no joy in giving if you give because you have to or because you feel guilty if you don't give. In that case, giving will probably just make you angry. Cheerful giving is more than throwing money into the plate. It is motive more than money.

Implications and Actions

Are you complete in the grace of giving? Maybe God has gifted you in many ways, but like the Corinthians, you are lacking in this area. Christians cannot experience the full joy of the Christian life unless they are complete in the area of giving.

Giving, however, starts not with the pocketbook but by giving ourselves. Once we truly give ourselves, giving money becomes a joy because we realize how blessed we are to invest in the work of God's kingdom. When we give, we are able to look around at all God is doing and know that we have a part in something that is bigger than ourselves.

So give, but not out of guilt or coercion. Do not give with the motive of greed, thinking that if you give money you will get more money back. Give out of gratitude for the gift that God has given to us in Jesus Christ. Giving is not just a part of the gospel; it is the heart of the gospel.

QUESTIONS

1. Consider this statement: *Christian giving is not about how much I should give; it is about how much I should keep.* Do you agree or disagree? Why or why not?

2. Do you find giving to be joyful or painful?

3. Think about your pattern of giving. Do you give in a regular, systematic way, or do you give if you have something left over?

4. What do you think would be the practical consequences if Christians suddenly stopped giving to their local church? What would be the spiritual consequences?

5. What would be the consequences to your church if everyone in it reflected your attitude toward giving and your giving patterns?

6. How do you think the Corinthians responded to Paul's appeal to give? How would you have responded?

Acts 20:7-12
Mark 1:21-34

FOCAL TEXT
Mark 1:35–36;
Luke 4:16; 11:1–4;
Philippians 4:6

BACKGROUND
Mark 1:35–36;
Luke 4:16; 11:1–13;
Philippians 4:6

MAIN IDEA
The example and instruction of Jesus teach us that Christians should worship both privately and together.

QUESTION TO EXPLORE
How important is worship to you?

STUDY AIM
To commit myself to worship privately and with fellow believers

QUICK READ
Jesus worshiped both in private and in public. Furthermore, he taught his disciples how to worship. Jesus' example continues to instruct both private and public Christian worship practices.

LESSON SEVEN
The Discipline of Worship

In the last few years I have been hearing a phrase that I consider to be an oxymoron, *worship wars*. The phrase refers to a clash of cultures resulting in church arguments over the appropriate style of worship. Some want traditional worship that holds on to traditional hymns, complete with organ music. Others want contemporary music with praise bands and guitars. Some want freedom and spontaneity, while others prefer a highly-controlled script with written prayers and predetermined liturgies. While I understand the meaning of the phrase, *worship wars* seems ironic at best and contradictory at worst.

Think about the most meaningful worship experiences in which you have participated. Several years ago, I went on a mission trip to Brazil. The little church in which I was preaching used drums and guitars. The people packed into the small building and sang their hearts out. They prayed with fervor and lifted their hands in praise. That God's Spirit was in that place was evident. They knew how to worship not only with their voices but with every ounce of their being. I thought, *This is what worship is supposed to be.*

Recently I went to England. While there, I worshiped in the Anglican tradition at Canterbury Cathedral. When I walked into the cathedral, I was instantly aware of an awesome presence as I realized that believers had been worshiping in this place for well over 1,000 years. The high ceiling reminded me of the transcendence of God Almighty. The acoustics reverberated with a mysterious echo. The worship service was highly scripted. We read from the *Book of Common Prayer*, and the choir sang psalms that echoed off the stone walls. No one moved except to kneel when the order of service told us to kneel. Surrounded by such beautiful music and majestic architecture, clearly the Spirit of God was in that place. I thought, *This is what worship is supposed to be.*

I find myself able to worship in both styles. What is authentic worship? How do we know it when we see it? Whether we sing, pray, give, or preach, worship is directed to God and is for God.

MARK 1:35–36

35Very early in the morning, while it was still dark, Jesus got up, left the house and went off to a solitary place, where he prayed. 36Simon and his companions went to look for him. . . .

LUKE 4:16

[16]He went to Nazareth, where he had been brought up, and on the Sabbath day he went into the synagogue, as was his custom. And he stood up to read.

LUKE 11:1–4

[1]One day Jesus was praying in a certain place. When he finished, one of his disciples said to him, "Lord, teach us to pray, just as John taught his disciples."
[2]He said to them, "When you pray, say:
"'Father,
hallowed be your name,
your kingdom come.
[3] Give us each day our daily bread.
[4] Forgive us our sins,
for we also forgive everyone who sins against us.
And lead us not into temptation.'"

PHILIPPIANS 4:6

[6]Do not be anxious about anything, but in everything, by prayer and petition, with thanksgiving, present your requests to God.

Jesus Worshiped in Private (Mark 1:35–36)

Mark portrayed Jesus in constant action. Jesus had called his first disciples, driven an evil spirit out of a man, healed Simon Peter's mother-in-law, and ministered to a crowd of people who came to him after dark.

Jesus kept very busy, but early in the morning he found time to get away from the hustle and bustle of ministry to pray. Prayer is one discipline of worship that Jesus demonstrated. You get the feeling that Jesus needed that time to be prepared for the busy day to come. If Jesus needed to worship privately, how much more do we?

The Bible says that Jesus went to a solitary place where he would be alone. A "solitary place" literally means a *wilderness place*. On the one hand, it refers to a place where Jesus could go where no one would find him. But Simon and his companions eventually found Jesus and prodded him back into busyness. But for a few moments, Jesus was alone with the Father.

But a *wilderness place* also carries dark overtones. The phrase recalls the time when Jesus was in the desert being tempted by Satan. There Jesus threw off the temptations to be a popular, political messiah and determined instead to follow God's will as a Suffering Servant. Now, once again, Jesus was alone in a solitary place following a busy day of healing among adoring crowds. Perhaps Jesus needed to worship to refocus his attention on why he came. He came to preach about the kingdom. He came to suffer and die. This time of worship must have served to focus Jesus on his mission and to continue to ward off the temptation to be a physical and political savior. Jesus came away to this time of private worship, once again turning away from the acclamation of the crowds in order to refocus on his main mission.

Private worship helps us focus on God's will for our lives. Through our private worship, God's Spirit reveals God's mission to us. Private prayer and worship remind us of God's will and lead us away from temptation.

VARIETIES OF WORSHIP STYLES AMONG BAPTISTS

Christians throughout the centuries have worshiped God in a variety of ways. Some Christians observe the Lord's Supper every week while others observe it occasionally. Quakers often worship together in total silence until the Spirit moves someone in the congregation to speak a word from the Lord. Anglican worship is very formal, with a set liturgy that seldom varies, while Pentecostal worship is free and spontaneous.

Baptist worship has been influenced by traditions of form and order as well as freedom for the movement of the Spirit. You can find different forms of worship in Baptist churches all over the world.

Try a study of different worship traditions. What traditions do you think have influenced the worship in your church?

Jesus Worshiped in Public (Luke 4:16)

Not only did Jesus worship in private, but he also worshiped in public. Worshiping in solitude is a very important discipline that enhances our spiritual life. But if we do not also participate in corporate worship, we are depriving ourselves of a vital spiritual experience that cannot be replicated elsewhere.

The Scripture tells us of a particular Sabbath when Jesus went to the synagogue in his hometown of Nazareth. This was his *home church,* so to speak. It was hardly the first time he had been among these people. He had known them all his life. They were his friends and family. He chose this setting of corporate worship to announce the commencement of his ministry.

The Bible indicates that Jesus was in the habit of attending corporate worship. This was not a onetime experience but was the culmination of a lifetime of worship with the people he knew well.

Jesus participated in worship not only by his attendance, but also in a leadership role as he stood to read the Scripture. Although on this occasion his friends and family reacted negatively to his sermon, Jesus nevertheless understood the importance of worship in a corporate setting.

Occasionally someone will tell me they can worship God just as well on the lake or on the golf course. While I suppose it is possible to worship on the golf course, I doubt it really happens. Private worship is important, as stated earlier. But if we do not come together with the people of God in corporate worship, our Christian experience is woefully incomplete. Corporate worship is indispensable for the Christian. Without it we cannot participate in the mission of the church, which is to glorify God. When God's people worship together, the Spirit of God is present in a unique way, working in our lives.

Jesus gave us the example of corporate worship. We would be foolish not to participate with the body of Christ in that most important and unique moment.

Jesus Taught His Disciples to Worship (Luke 11:1–4)

Not only did Jesus worship privately and publicly, but he also taught his disciples how to worship, particularly the discipline of prayer. On this occasion it seems that as Jesus prayed with his disciples present, his prayer motivated them to ask questions about prayer. They wanted Jesus to teach them to pray. It was not an uncommon request. Students often asked their rabbi to teach them to pray. Jesus gave us a model for all time.

A mother heard her little girl reciting the alphabet in a very reverent tone. "What are you doing?" the mother asked.

"I'm praying," the little girl said. "I can't think of exactly the right words so I am just saying all of the letters and God will put them together for me."

While such childlike faith is encouraging, Jesus helped us to think of the right words. He taught his disciples a model prayer that continues to serve as a model for all believers in all times.

Prayer and worship begin by acknowledging the holy nature of God. The word "hallowed" means that God is sacred and set apart from all other beings. In worship we may express this truth in hymns of praise.

Jesus then asked that God's kingdom would come. This happens when the people of this world order their lives around God's mission and purpose.

Jesus continued by acknowledging our need for God in this world. He asked God to give us the things we need for physical life on a daily basis.

But we need more than physical sustenance. We need forgiveness. God stands ready to forgive, but we must recognize the need to forgive others. Forgiveness has both spiritual and social dimensions. Since God forgives us, we too must forgive those who have hurt us. We forgive because we have experienced God's forgiveness.

Finally, Jesus said we should pray for God to help us when tempted. God stands ready to give us strength to resist temptation so that we will not fall into sin.

Jesus' prayer provides us with a helpful model for worship, whether we are worshiping privately or publicly. Worship should include praise, petition, confession, forgiveness, and encouragement that we may stand strong against temptation.

Jesus' teaching his disciples speaks to the tremendous responsibility we have to teach people of all ages how to worship. Worship leaders, teachers, and especially parents have a wonderful opportunity each week to train others to worship. Pastors and ministers of music have a responsibility to teach congregations by modeling theologically-sound worship patterns. Parents have a great opportunity because, as children watch their parents worship, they will ask questions about the things they see happening.

Jesus taught us how to worship. Now we have the opportunity to teach others.

Don't Worry, Just Worship (Philippians 4:6)

Ruth Bell Graham has received credit for this quote: "Worship and worry cannot live in the same heart; they are mutually exclusive." Two thousand years earlier the Apostle Paul said something similar. He told the Philippians to be "anxious for nothing." That was quite a statement to make to the Philippians, who had a lot to worry about. They were in economic distress and experiencing persecution.

Paul said that they should pray and worship. They should express their fears to God and ask for their daily needs to be met. They should worship with thanksgiving. They should boldly make their requests to the Lord. Then they could leave their anxiety in God's hands.

Worshiping God eliminates any reason to be anxious because our worship expresses our trust in God. If we continue to be anxious, we have betrayed a lack of trust in God, and our worship is empty ritual. True worship results in total trust. True prayer and worship change us.

The movie *Shadowlands* portrays the story of C. S. (Jack) Lewis, the Christian author. In particular, it focuses on the terrible difficulties of Lewis and his wife Joy as Joy was suffering with cancer. At one point in the story a friend says to Lewis, "Jack, I know how hard you've been praying; and now God is answering your prayers." Lewis then says,

CASE STUDY

A couple in your Sunday School class has not been attending worship lately. When you ask them why, they answer, "We don't get anything out of worship. It doesn't meet our needs." What would you say to them?

"That's not why I pray, Harry. I pray because I can not help myself. I pray because I'm helpless. I pray because the need flows out of me all the time, waking and sleeping. It doesn't change God; it changes me."

As we learn to trust God in the ongoing disciplines of prayer and worship, we are changed. Worship eliminates worry because in true worship we learn to trust an almighty God.

Implications and Actions

Christians may and often do have strong opinions regarding styles of worship. That's to be expected. But personal preferences should create neither hostility nor animosity between worshipers. Worship is a unifying discipline of the Christian faith.

Style is not the real issue. The real issue is that, for many people, worship is about themselves and their own desires. But worship, whether private or corporate, is not about us. Worship is about God. Worship should lead us to acknowledge God's holiness, to long for God's coming kingdom, to trust that God will provide, to delight in forgiveness, and to plead for strength to help us live godly lives.

As you attend worship services, seek out those moments that have been designed to lead us into true worship of God. Give yourself to God. Don't worry, just worship.

QUESTIONS

1. How often do you practice private worship? When would be the best time for you in a busy schedule to be alone with God?

2. What practices can you think of to use in your times of private worship?

3. Study the order of worship provided by your church. Where are the opportunities you have to praise God, to trust God, to confess sin and rejoice in forgiveness, and to pray for strength?

4. Do you and your family worship together? Think of teachable moments when you can teach your children or grandchildren about worship.

5. How can you help people in your church to understand the
    advantages of diversity in styles of public worship?

FOCAL TEXT
Matthew 18:15–17, 21–35;
2 Corinthians 2:5–11

BACKGROUND
Matthew 18:15–35;
2 Corinthians 2:5–11

MAIN IDEA
Following Christ calls
believers to relate to
one another with open
communication, a concern
for the church as a whole,
and a willingness to forgive.

QUESTION TO EXPLORE
How can church members
develop and maintain
Christlike relationships
with one another?

STUDY AIM
To commit myself to Christlike
ways of relating to other people

QUICK READ
The gospel reconciles people
to God and to one another.
When there is a broken
relationship with another
believer, the relationship needs
to be restored. Jesus and Paul
gave us models for reconciling
with one another and restoring
Christlike relationships.

LESSON EIGHT
The Discipline of Christlike Relationships

Tomas Borge was a freedom fighter for the Sandinistas in Nicaragua. While fighting a totalitarian regime, he was imprisoned, tortured, forced to wear a hood over his head for nine months, and endured the rape of his wife by his enemies. Borge was freed after the revolution and became the Minister of the Interior for the new government. While we might not agree with Borge's political philosophy, his practical theology was stunning. He faced his torturers in the courtroom, and the court allowed him to name the kind of revenge he wanted to inflict on them. As Borge looked his enemies in the eyes, he replied, "My revenge is to forgive you."[1]

Borge's attitude seems almost unbelievable. How could a person possibly forgive someone who had done so much damage? In this world, particularly in the realm of revolutionary politics, the natural and expected reaction of such a victim would be to inflict as much pain as possible on the perpetrator. Yet, even in this secular and revolutionary context, Tomas Borge was ready to forgive.

Relationships between Christians are even more important than political relationships. Yet often we find relationships in the church strained or broken because of some offense against a fellow believer. Christian relationships suffer because someone was accosted in the parking lot or heard a word of offense in the hallway. Sometimes fellow believers are ripped apart because of a business deal that went bad. They come to church on Sunday morning, sit in the same room to worship and share communion, but leave church without finding it possible to forgive and reconcile.

Jesus commanded his followers to be reconciled with one another. He then offered specific instructions about how to be reconciled. Jesus insisted on open communication, a concern for the unity of the church, and a willingness to forgive. Furthermore, Paul provided an excellent example from a situation in the Corinthian church about how to forgive someone who has offended you. If a Communist revolutionary like Tomas Borge can forgive someone who tortured him and raped his wife, then Jesus' disciples should be able to forgive even more.

A Prescription for Relationship Repair (Matthew 18:15–17)

Relationships, even in church, are complicated ventures that carry with them tremendous possibility for conflict. Conflict has the power to

MATTHEW 18:15–17, 21–35

[15]"If your brother sins against you, go and show him his fault, just between the two of you. If he listens to you, you have won your brother over. [16]But if he will not listen, take one or two others along, so that 'every matter may be established by the testimony of two or three witnesses.' [17]If he refuses to listen to them, tell it to the church; and if he refuses to listen even to the church, treat him as you would a pagan or a tax collector.

. . . .

[21]Then Peter came to Jesus and asked, "Lord, how many times shall I forgive my brother when he sins against me? Up to seven times?"

[22]Jesus answered, "I tell you, not seven times, but seventy-seven times.

[23]"Therefore, the kingdom of heaven is like a king who wanted to settle accounts with his servants. [24]As he began the settlement, a man who owed him ten thousand talents was brought to him. [25]Since he was not able to pay, the master ordered that he and his wife and his children and all that he had be sold to repay the debt.

[26]"The servant fell on his knees before him. 'Be patient with me,' he begged, 'and I will pay back everything.' [27]The servant's master took pity on him, canceled the debt and let him go.

[28]"But when that servant went out, he found one of his fellow servants who owed him a hundred denarii. He grabbed him and began to choke him. 'Pay back what you owe me!' he demanded.

[29]"His fellow servant fell to his knees and begged him, 'Be patient with me, and I will pay you back.'

[30]"But he refused. Instead, he went off and had the man thrown into prison until he could pay the debt. [31]When the other servants saw what had happened, they were greatly distressed and went and told their master everything that had happened.

[32]"Then the master called the servant in. 'You wicked servant,' he said, 'I canceled all that debt of yours because you begged me to. [33]Shouldn't you have had mercy on your fellow servant just as I

had on you?' [34]In anger his master turned him over to the jailers to be tortured, until he should pay back all he owed.

[35]"This is how my heavenly Father will treat each of you unless you forgive your brother from your heart."

2 CORINTHIANS 2:5–11

[5]If anyone has caused grief, he has not so much grieved me as he has grieved all of you, to some extent—not to put it too severely. [6]The punishment inflicted on him by the majority is sufficient for him. [7]Now instead, you ought to forgive and comfort him, so that he will not be overwhelmed by excessive sorrow. [8]I urge you, therefore, to reaffirm your love for him. [9]The reason I wrote you was to see if you would stand the test and be obedient in everything. [10]If you forgive anyone, I also forgive him. And what I have forgiven—if there was anything to forgive—I have forgiven in the sight of Christ for your sake, [11]in order that Satan might not outwit us. For we are not unaware of his schemes.

damage relationships. While damaged relationships sometimes result from simple misunderstanding, torn relationships can also result from one person sinning against another. Jesus understood that since his followers live in an imperfect world, broken relationships among them were inevitable. But even though we live in this world, we also live in the kingdom of God. Our relationships with one another ought to be kingdom relationships. Those relationships must be harmonious in order to show the world that following Jesus offers a different way to live.

How should Jesus' disciples restore and repair broken relationships? Jesus gave us a prescription that stresses love as a motive with restoration as the desired result.

First, Jesus said that if someone has sinned against you, you have the responsibility to take the initiative in restoring the relationship. The process of reconciliation begins with the action of the one who was sinned against. It is not that the sinner has no responsibility, but the person who has sinned may be impaired from the ability to take the initiative. The wronged person is often in a better position to initiate reconciliation.

The first attempt to restore a broken relationship should be in private without public humiliation or exposure. The motive should be to restore the relationship, not to embarrass or punish the offender. If the offender is willing to be reconciled, there is no reason to make it a public affair or even speak of it again.

However, the person may refuse to be reconciled by a private plea. In that case the offended person should take one or two other people from the church to discuss the matter with the offender. Jesus quoted from Deuteronomy 19:15 when he spoke these words. The law was concerned with having sufficient evidence in a court of law. Witnesses would be able to establish the nature of the offense and determine whether the offense was true. Perhaps, too, the hope was that the witnesses could help mediate reconciliation between the estranged parties.

If reconciliation still did not occur, it became a church matter because a broken relationship affected the unity of the church. Note the sense of accountability in this difficult step. Disciples of Jesus are accountable to one another. If a ruptured relationship exists in the church, the church must take responsibility for maintaining church unity. If the offender still does not desire reconciliation, the church must recognize that the person is refusing fellowship with the church. This is a grievous moment for any church body when they realize that a person has chosen to exclude himself or herself from Christian fellowship.

The possibility for reconciliation still remains after the person has excluded himself or herself. But at this point it becomes the responsibility of the offender to take the initiative for reconciling. When that happens, the church should be ready to forgive and restore the person to fellowship.

The Key to Relationship Repair (Matthew 18:21–35)

The key to reconciliation is forgiveness. There can be no restoration if we cannot forgive someone who has wronged us.

Peter asked Jesus, *How many times should I forgive my brother? Seven times?* Peter thought he was being very generous since the Jewish rabbis taught that people should forgive three times but not the fourth time. Peter doubled the requirement and then added another time for good measure.

Jesus had taught the disciples to pray, *Forgive us our debts in the same way we forgive our debtors.* Do we want God to forgive us only seven times? I need more forgiveness than that.

Jesus answered that we should forgive without keeping count.[2] Jesus was not putting a number on the times we ought to forgive but was saying that forgiveness should be infinite. We must place no limits on how often we forgive a brother or sister who sins against us. In this world, revenge is unlimited. In the kingdom of heaven, forgiveness is unlimited.

Jesus told a story to illustrate the principle of forgiveness. A king forgave a man for a debt of 10,000 talents. This sum was tremendous, amounting to about 60,000,000 denarii by one estimate. Since a denarius was the equivalent of a day's wage for a laborer, the man would have had to work 60 million days just to pay his debt. What a gift!

When the forgiven debtor went back on the street, he saw another man who owed him 100 denarii. The man pleaded for delay but was refused. In fact, the man who had been forgiven by the king had his debtor thrown into prison until he could repay. Of course he would never be able to repay since he was in prison and unable to work. When the king heard about this injustice, he took the first man and not only put him in prison but gave him over to torturers to be tortured until he paid back the 10,000 talents.

God's mercy is unlimited. He forgives the great debt of sin. How can we then refuse to forgive someone who has sinned against us?

LAMECH AND VENGEANCE

In Genesis 4:19–24 a man named Lamech is mentioned. He said to his wives, Adah and Zillah, "I have killed a man for wounding me, and young man for injuring me. If Cain is avenged seven times, then Lamech seventy-seven times." Thus Lamech expressed this world's attitude of vengeance. He was stating that revenge was unlimited.

When Peter asked Jesus how many times he should forgive, Peter suggested seven times. Peter believed he was being generous. Maybe he had the story of Lamech in mind. Perhaps Jesus also was recalling the story of Lamech as he noted that we should forgive seventy-seven times. Jesus certainly reversed the law of vengeance that Lamech had expressed. Instead of unlimited revenge, a follower of Jesus must practice unlimited forgiveness.

The world was aghast in the aftermath of the shooting perpetrated by a crazed gunman in an Amish schoolhouse. Students were lined up and shot. Rarely has such an atrocity been committed. But the world stood amazed when reporters interviewed the Amish. While there was tremendous sadness, there was also forgiveness. The Amish forgave the gunman and visited and comforted the shooter's wife. Some even attended his funeral. Their gracious actions spoke volumes to a world that often seeks revenge. They showed unlimited forgiveness. Their actions and words were an incredible witness to the gospel of Jesus Christ. God was glorified because they forgave. Most of us will never have to forgive in circumstances like the Amish shooting. But they have shown us a wonderful example of Jesus' teaching on forgiveness.

An Example of Relationship Repair (2 Corinthians 2:5–11)

Someone in the Corinthian church evidently had done something to offend Paul. The exact nature of the offense is impossible to determine. Some scholars have speculated that the offense may be related to the man Paul condemned in 1 Corinthians 5, but no certain evidence indicates that Paul was addressing that issue here. Whatever the case, someone had perpetrated a grievous offense against Paul that had resulted in a disruption of relationships in the church.

The offense not only injured Paul but also damaged the church. Paul had written a *severe letter* to the church, evidently advising the church to discipline the man. This discipline had been carried out with vigor and may have resulted in even further disruption of church unity. A broken relationship has far-reaching effects. Not only does it hurt the person who sinned and the person sinned against, it hurts the entire community. This man's sin against Paul set off a chain of events that disrupted the unity of the whole church.

Paul insisted that the discipline inflicted on the man by the majority of the church was more than sufficient and that the time had come for restoration. In fact, a person might surmise from Paul's words that the Corinthian church may have gone overboard in their discipline, alienating not only the man but also others in the fellowship. He asked the church to forgive the offender and comfort him. Forgiveness is the passive attitude that makes reconciliation possible. But they were to go beyond forgiveness to actively comfort the man to assure him that he was restored to their fellowship.

The point of the discipline was twofold. First, it should have motivated the offending brother to repentance with the ultimate goal of full reconciliation with the church. Paul indicated that the brother was sufficiently sorrowful. It the church continued its harsh discipline, the man might be so overcome with sorrow that he would turn from his faith. The motive for church discipline is not punitive. Instead discipline's desire is repentance and restoration.

The second point of the discipline was to test the Corinthian church to see whether they were serious about the moral and ethical implications of the gospel. Paul wanted to see whether they would be obedient to his difficult request. Indeed they were obedient, maybe even more than Paul intended.

Church discipline is one of the most difficult parts of church life. However, sometimes it is necessary in order to continue a pure witness to the world and to maintain church unity.

Paul urged the whole church to forgive and comfort the man. Paul even took the first step, saying that he had already forgiven him, not only for the sake of the man but for the sake of the church. Forgiving and restoring the man to the fellowship of the church would not only reconcile the man to the church but would reconcile the majority and minority factions in the fellowship.

If reconciliation did not occur, Paul feared that they would be playing into the hands of Satan. One of the schemes of the Evil One is to divide the church over matters that could be resolved if the church would forgive one another. With Christlike relationships in place, the church is

CASE STUDY

Ben, Jerry, and Jerry's wife Mary attend the same church. Ben made an inappropriate comment to Mary and even suggested some inappropriate behavior. Jerry and Mary were rightfully offended. The offense resulted in a rift of their relationship. Jerry and Mary are contemplating leaving the church. What should they do? What would you do if you were Jerry or Mary? What actions should the church take?

better able to accomplish its purpose despite Satan's efforts to thwart those plans.

Implications and Actions

Healthy, Christlike relationships are crucial for the well-being of the church and for it to maintain a positive witness to the world. Broken relationships are sinful. Jesus came to reconcile people to God and people to one another. If we refuse to be reconciled to one another, we are denying the gospel and thwarting the purpose of Christ's coming.

On a personal level, we have all experienced divided relationships in one way or another. You may have been offended by a person in your church. Sometimes we just sweep the problem under the rug and never attempt to solve it. We think the problem will go away if we just ignore it. But the relationship is broken, even if the offense is suffered in silence. The gospel demands that we not live in suffering silence but be reconciled to our brother or sister by taking positive action.

The task of reconciliation demands forgiveness and comfort. Not only must we find forgiveness in our hearts, but we must pursue actions that assure our brothers and sisters that the relationship is fully restored. God's grace in us empowers us to accomplish this difficult but necessary work.

Sometimes the church must exercise church discipline. Such discipline always should have the goal of restoration to the fellowship. It should never be punitive or designed to embarrass. It should seek repentance on the part of the offender, forgiveness on the part of the church, and reconciliation as its ultimate goal.

QUESTIONS

1. How do you normally respond when someone offends you? Do you respond in a Christlike or an ungodly manner?

2. Under what circumstances do you think a church should practice church discipline? What would be involved in disciplining a member of the church? What procedure should the church follow?

3. Is there anyone in your church family that you have been unable to forgive? What steps do you need to take to restore the relationship? Are you willing to take the steps necessary to restore that relationship?

4. How effective would church discipline be in our society when a person excluded from the church simply drives to another nearby church and unites with it?

NOTES

1. Simon Wiesenthal, "The Sunflower: On the Possibilities and Limits of Forgiveness," Schocken Books, 1997, p. 123. (See also Tomas Borge, *Christianity and Revolution: Tomas Borge's Theology of Life*, Orbis Books, Maryknoll, NY, 1987.)

2. The NIV says seventy-seven times. Other translations translate the phrase seventy times seven. Both are possible. Jesus was not concerned about keeping a tally but on the need to offer unlimited forgiveness.

FOCAL TEXT
Colossians 3:1–14

BACKGROUND
Colossians 2:20—3:14

MAIN IDEA
Because of Christians'
relationship with Christ, they
are to stop living in ways
that bring dishonor to Christ
and start living in ways that
bring honor to Christ.

QUESTION TO EXPLORE
What difference does Christ
make in how you live each day?

STUDY AIM
To decide on at least one
change I will make in the way
I live so as to honor Christ

QUICK READ
Followers of Jesus have died
to the old way of life. A true
disciple lives in a manner
that reflects a new way of
life that is focused on the
kingdom of God rather than
the ways of this world.

LESSON NINE
The Discipline of Right Living

Think back on a person whom you have met who changed your life from the moment you met. The result may have come as a total surprise. Perhaps you did not even know when you met the person that your life would never be the same.

I remember well the moment I first met my wife. It was the first day of my junior year in college. It was Wednesday, and I went to church as was my normal custom on Wednesday evenings. I was standing in line to get a plateful of food at our fellowship dinner, and she was standing in front of me. She turned around and introduced herself. Little did I know that introduction would change the entire course of my life.

After meeting her, my view of the world changed. I no longer looked at other girls as prospective brides. I didn't want to spend time doing the things I had done before. I wanted to spend time with her. Eventually, I was ready to make a lifetime commitment to her before God. I would renounce all other relationships, and my time would be devoted to a family. We made that public commitment to each other at our wedding. We have now been married more than twenty years, and my life has never been like it was before I met her.

When we meet Jesus, life can never be the same as it was before we met him. Before meeting Jesus our lives revolved around the things of this world. We concentrated on worldly things that we thought would benefit us. But when we met Jesus, our view of the world changed. When we were baptized, we publicly committed to renounce the old way of life. We are no longer to be focused on ourselves, but to focus on Christ. We no longer see things the way we did, and neither do we live the way we did. In fact, being a disciple of Jesus compels us toward righteous living.

COLOSSIANS 3:1–14

¹Since, then, you have been raised with Christ, set your hearts on things above, where Christ is seated at the right hand of God. ²Set your minds on things above, not on earthly things. ³For you died, and your life is now hidden with Christ in God. ⁴When Christ, who is your life, appears, then you also will appear with him in glory.

⁵Put to death, therefore, whatever belongs to your earthly nature: sexual immorality, impurity, lust, evil desires and greed,

which is idolatry. [6]Because of these, the wrath of God is coming. [7]You used to walk in these ways, in the life you once lived. [8]But now you must rid yourselves of all such things as these: anger, rage, malice, slander, and filthy language from your lips. [9]Do not lie to each other, since you have taken off your old self with its practices [10]and have put on the new self, which is being renewed in knowledge in the image of its Creator. [11]Here there is no Greek or Jew, circumcised or uncircumcised, barbarian, Scythian, slave or free, but Christ is all, and is in all.

[12]Therefore, as God's chosen people, holy and dearly loved, clothe yourselves with compassion, kindness, humility, gentleness and patience. [13]Bear with each other and forgive whatever grievances you may have against one another. Forgive as the Lord forgave you. [14]And over all these virtues put on love, which binds them all together in perfect unity.

Don't Look Back (2:20–23)

The background text for this lesson reminds us of the situation Paul was addressing when he wrote to the Colossians. They had committed themselves to Christ and accepted the gospel of grace that Paul proclaimed. However, it seems that false teachers had infiltrated the church and were encouraging the church members to go back to some of the rules and regulations that they had relied on before they became Christians.

The particular heresy that was being taught by the false teachers in Colossae is hard to pin down. The letter to the church gives us some clues. The false teaching had some elements that have been identified with the Judaizers. Judaizers believed that a person had to become a Jew and follow the Jewish law before becoming a Christian. The false teaching also had some elements of Gnostic thought. Gnostics believed that material things were evil while spiritual things were good. Since material things were evil, some people felt free to abuse their bodies because they saw no connection between the health of the body and that of the spirit.

These false teachers encouraged the Colossian Christians to go back to their old way of life, relying on works of the flesh instead of the grace of God. Paul told them not to look back or to revert to how they were before they met Christ. Meeting Christ had changed everything for them. They could not go back to the way things were before.

Raised to a New Life (3:1–4)

Paul reminded the Colossians that they had been "raised up" with Christ in baptism. In the NIV, Colossians 3:1 begins, "Since, therefore, you have been raised. . . ." The word "since" is a good translation of the meaning in the Greek. There was no uncertainty in Paul's mind that the Colossians had made a commitment to Christ. They had declared their commitment at their baptism.

Paul used the baptism motif to describe what had happened to the Colossians when they met Jesus. They had died with Christ and been raised with him in their baptism (2:12). Because of this real experience with Christ, their aim in life had changed. They saw things in a new light. Their minds were focused on the things of Christ instead of the things of this world.

Paul was also alluding to the ascension of Jesus. Jesus ascended to heaven, and in like manner, the Colossian believers had ascended above the things of this world so that their perspective changed. Followers of Jesus no longer see things the way they used to see them when their minds focused on the things of this world. Now they see things from a heavenly standpoint. If believers can see things from the standpoint of God's kingdom, why do we still focus our minds on the things of this world?

The old person, before meeting Jesus, is dead. The commitment we make to Christ eliminates the person that we were. Life is never the same again.

The new person is very much alive in Christ, and Paul described the new life as hidden in Christ. The pagans used to speak of death as a hiding in the earth, but Christians claim to be hidden in Christ. The Christian life is beyond this world's understanding because it cannot see or know Christ. But the life of the Christian already belongs to the yet-to-be-revealed realm of God's kingdom.

THE COLOSSIAN HERESY

Scholars have scratched their heads over the details of the false teaching that was going on in Colosse. The false teaching seems to have had elements of two problems the early church faced.

Judaizers were believers in Jesus, but they insisted that a person had to become a Jew before the person could be saved by Jesus. This would include observing the Jewish dietary regulations, observing certain holidays, and submitting to circumcision. This had been a subject of contention in the church since the earliest days of the church and is noted especially at the Jerusalem Council (Acts 15:1–29).

Gnosticism was also an element in the Colossian heresy. Gnostics believed all material things were evil but spiritual things were good. In order to progress in the spiritual world one had to have knowledge of certain secret mysteries. Because physical things were considered evil, some Gnostics abused their bodies as punishment of evil. Others lived immoral lifestyles since they believed that anything one did with one's body did not affect the spirit. This heresy did not reach its full manifestation until the second century, but the New Testament is full of arguments against an early version of Gnosticism that was creeping into churches.

The yet-to-be-revealed aspect of the kingdom will be revealed someday when Christ will return and make himself known to the world. His followers will be with him. Then everyone will see Christ for who he really is.

The Christian life is to be so filled up with Christ that its aim, its mind, and its hope are taken up with Jesus. The secret to the discipline of right living is not obsession with the negatives of this world but obsession with the living Christ. If we are completely filled up with Christ, there is no room for obsession with the things of this world.

Things to Remove (3:5–11)

The person you were before you met Christ is dead. What does the new raised-up person look like? Paul said to "put to death" everything that belongs to the worldly nature. He gave the Colossians a list of examples of things he was talking about. The list is not exhaustive but instructive.

First, Paul mentioned sins of a sexual nature. God's gift of sex is wonderful when used as intended within the boundaries of marriage. The abuse of God's gift of sex clearly indicates that a person's mind is focused on self-gratification rather than self-giving love. The words Paul used indicate that the abuse of sex stems from minds that are focused on this world rather than God's world.

The next sin Paul mentioned was "greed," the sin of coveting that the tenth commandment condemns. Coveting means desiring to have something that you have no right to have. Coveting applies to the whole range of worldly desires. Paul said coveting is nothing more than idolatry because the desire to obtain worldly things is, in fact, worshiping false gods. Paul warned the Colossians, and all followers of Jesus, that God's wrath comes upon the idolatrous.

Paul provided a second list of things that belong to the worldly nature. He told the Colossians, "You must rid yourselves of all such things." Here Paul used a metaphor of changing clothes. Figuratively, the clothes that the Christians had worn before they met Christ were dirty and torn. *Take them off,* Paul told them. This probably continues the baptism motif introduced earlier. Some scholars think that when people were baptized in the early church they took off their old clothes and were given a new set of white clothing that symbolized their new, pure life when they came up out of the waters. Paul seemed to use this picture to demonstrate some of the worldly things believers should shed.

The things Paul listed have to do with relationships that we have with one another, particularly as they relate to words that come from our mouths. Anger, rage, malice, slander, and filthy language have no place for the disciple whose mind is on "things above." Furthermore, Paul condemned lying to one another. All these things are a part of the old way of life because they are focused on oneself rather than the well-being of others. These sins destroy relationships between believers.

It is interesting to note that Paul equated this second list of sins with the sexual sins in the first list. We often take great offense at sexual immorality but seldom blink at someone who gossips or holds a grudge. Nevertheless, the sins of attitude and speech are every bit a part of the old way of life as are sexual sins. All of these things should be shed from the Christian life because they are part of the old life before we met Christ.

Things to Put On (3:10–14)

Disciples of Jesus should put on righteous living that is worthy of the Christ they proclaim. Paul said that the Colossians had already put on the new self. This is the exact opposite of what he mentioned in Colossians 3:5. The new "clothes" that a Christian has put on represent an ongoing and radical change in ethical direction.

Right living means that we should behave as God originally created us to behave. We should be in fellowship with God and with each other. This kind of living recognizes that all people are created in God's image. In this new world, there are no social barriers that hold us back as in the old world. Racism, hatred, and prejudice are part of the old life and should be discarded.

Paul gave other examples of right living. Christians should clothe themselves with compassion, kindness, humility, gentleness, and patience. These things belong to the new life that Christians have put on. They are the opposite of the old life because they are concerned with the well-being of others rather than self.

Perhaps the most telling attribute of the new clothes a believer wears is the practice of forgiveness. We are told over and over again in the New Testament, especially in the teachings of Jesus, that we should forgive in the same way God has forgiven us. Paul reiterated that truth by encouraging Christians to bear with one another and forgive one another. If believers would forgive one another in the same way that God forgives us, there would be no anger, slander, or grudges. Forgiveness goes a long way toward right living.

BAPTISM AND A CHANGED LIFE

Your friend declared her faith in Jesus and was baptized last Sunday. However, she is still living the highly questionable way she did before she was saved. What could you do to help her realize that meeting Jesus is intended to change everything about her life?

Finally, Paul said to cover all of these virtues with love. Love should be like a coat or a wrap that covers everything else. He may even have had in mind a garment that holds everything together. Love is not an emotion but is an action based on a commitment to always do what is best for another person. Love gathers up all of the virtues of right living and motivates us to live according to the *new clothes* we put on when we were baptized.

Implications and Actions

Being a Christian is not merely a one-time event that happened when we accepted Jesus as Savior. Rather it is a radical change of life. Meeting Jesus means that things can never be the same for us.

Sometimes Baptists have put such an emphasis on *walking the aisle to get saved* that we neglect the discipline of right living. But being a follower of Jesus means that our whole life is different because we have changed our perspective from looking at things from the standpoint of this world to looking at things from God's standpoint.

Baptism publicly signifies this radical change of life. Baptism is the event in which we symbolically shed the old life and put on the new life. We occasionally return to the old life, but it makes no sense for a baptized believer to return there. It is like having a new set of clothes that are clean and well-tailored, but instead we put on old clothes that are dirty and no longer fit. The only sensible thing for baptized believers to do is to live according to the new life God has given.

QUESTIONS

1. What are some things that have changed about your life since you met Christ? What are some things that have not changed but need to change?

2. Paul lists several examples of things that are a part of the old life. Can you think of other things from that life that Paul does not mention but should be shed from the Christian's life?

3. Paul lists several examples of things that are a part of the new life. Can you think of other things that should be put on as virtues that Paul does not mention?

4. Of the virtues that Paul mentioned in verses 12–14, which is the
   most difficult for you to practice?

Growing Together

In a single day, the New Testament church grew by a multiple of twenty-six. Before Pentecost, Acts tells us there were about 120 believers in the church (Acts 1:15). After Peter's sermon, this diverse congregation numbered 3,120 (Acts 1:15; 2:41). How does a church handle that kind of numerical growth? Luke painted a marvelous portrait of life in the first church in Acts 2:42–47. In these five lessons, we will study this passage along with a number of other New Testament passages to understand how a church not only grows but grows together.

Without question, the early church experienced considerable excitement. But the church is best characterized by the word *commitment*. Twice in his description of the church in Jerusalem, Luke uses the word *proskartero* to say that the believers "devoted" themselves (2:42) and "continued" to meet together (2:46). They expressed this commitment in five primary activities.

First, they placed a priority on Scripture as they devoted themselves to the apostles' teaching (2:42). Passages from Romans, 2 Timothy, and 2 Peter explain the development of the disciples' deep dependence on the Scriptures to enlighten their beliefs and their practices.

The disciples also devoted themselves to *koinonia* or fellowship, the sharing of their lives together (Acts 2:42–47). Paul's First Letter to the Corinthians paints a picture of the church as a body sharing the gifts God has given to the church. In his joyful letter to a church that brought him great joy, the church at Philippi, Paul exulted especially in the fellowship he shared with them as they shared the gospel together.

In Luke's summary in Acts 2:42–47, we also see the church at worship. The believers worshiped in awe and adoration, gladness and generosity. As they preached, prayed, ate the Lord's Supper, and sang, the early Christians gave God their minds' attention and their hearts' affection. Paul's teachings about the Lord's Supper (1 Corinthians 11:17–34) and about communicating through music (Ephesians 5:19–20) describe this picture of New Testament worship.

The early believers' discipleship, fellowship, and worship overflowed into the practical concern of meeting physical needs. Both inside and outside the church family, their love for Christ led them to love other people in practical ways. Paul's invitation to the Corinthians to make a special offering (1 Cor. 16:1–3) and James's teaching about proving faith by practical deeds of service (James 2:14–17) offer added insight to the ministry dimension of the early church.

What happens when a church teaches the Scriptures, fellowships together, worships regularly, and ministers to needs? In Jerusalem, the Lord "added to their number daily those who were being saved" (Acts 2:47). As the believers fulfilled the Great Commission (Matthew 28:18–20) and realized that Jesus had sent them into the world (John 20:19–21), they discovered that the gospel thrust them out into greater and greater concentric circles of concern. As Jesus had promised, the gospel spread all the way from the Jews in Jerusalem to the Samaritans to the Gentiles (Acts 11:19–26) who lived at the ends of the earth. As the believers did their part, God did his great work of salvation in the lives of those who believed.[1]

UNIT THREE, GROWING TOGETHER

Lesson 10	Place Priority on Scripture	Acts 2:42; Romans 15:4; 2 Timothy 3:14–17; 2 Peter 1:19–21
Lesson 11	Share Genuine Fellowship	Acts 2:42–47; 1 Corinthians 12:4–11; Philippians 1:3–9
Lesson 12	Worship Together	Acts 2:42–47; 1 Corinthians 11:17–34; Ephesians 5:19–20
Lesson 13	Minister to People's Needs	Acts 2:43–45; 3:1–8; 1 Corinthians 16:1–3; James 2:14–17
Lesson 14	Witness to the World	Acts 2:47b; Matthew 28:18–20; John 20:19–21; Acts 11:19–26

NOTES

1. Unless otherwise indicated, all Scripture quotations are from the New International Version.

FOCAL TEXT
Acts 2:42; Romans 15:4;
2 Timothy 3:14–17;
2 Peter 1:19–21

BACKGROUND
Acts 2:42–47;
Romans 15:4;
2 Timothy 3:14–17;
2 Peter 1:19–21

MAIN IDEA
A New Testament church and
its individual members are to
place priority on Scripture as
the basis for belief and practice.

QUESTION TO EXPLORE
How do you and your
church decide what to do?

STUDY AIM
To identify reasons Scripture
needs to be the basis for
my belief and practice

QUICK READ
What if the only part of the
Bible we really believe is
the part that we really live?
As the first church put the
apostles' teaching first, so
believers today must put the
Scriptures first so that we may
not only learn the Scriptures
but live according to them.

LESSON TEN
Place Priority on Scripture

My three brothers and I grew up in Germany as part of a military family. We always looked forward to the Christmas packages from our family in the United States. In particular, an aunt in Chicago, who was not at all wealthy, somehow always seemed to find the latest, greatest toys and gadgets to send to us. There were rockets with parachutes and the latest matchbox cars and tracks.

One year when I was about twelve years old, we opened the package. Immediately I realized she had made a mistake. Upon inspection of my wrapped gift, I discerned that instead of sending a toy, she had sent a book. I'll never forget the disappointment I felt in discovering my *Children's Living Bible* that morning. I envied my two older brothers who received a teen version of the same translation. What was I going to do with a Bible? Since we had no access to television, I decided the next summer to pick it up and read it. When I did I couldn't put it down. The Bible became a place for me to meet with God. Within a few years, I had surrendered to God's call into ministry.

Imagine the New Testament church. Right after Pentecost, the expanded group of believers needed guidance about what to do. Led by the Spirit, the apostles fulfilled the Great Commission by making disciples, baptizing the new believers, and teaching all things that Christ had taught them.

The first Christians committed themselves to first things first. The early believers first devoted themselves to the apostles' teachings (Acts 2:42). Consider how wonderful it must have been to hear Peter talk about being restored from personal failure, or Thomas talk about overcoming doubt, or John talk about loving Jesus. Those very teachings are available to us in the New Testament.

The apostles rooted their teachings in the Old Testament and in Jesus' teachings. One great example is found in Peter's sermon at Pentecost. There he quoted from the Old Testament again and again, interpreting God's work in the light of the Psalms and the Book of Joel. He also interpreted God's work through the lens of Jesus' life (Luke 24:27). Both the name and teaching of Jesus brought the conviction that led the people present at Pentecost to salvation (Acts 2:14–36).

As the first church put the apostles' teaching first, so believers today must put the Scriptures first so that we may not only learn the Scriptures but live according to them. So what exactly do the Scriptures do for us?

In the letters of Paul and Peter, we find New Testament teachings about the value of Scripture for faith and practice.

ACTS 2:42

42They devoted themselves to the apostles' teaching and to the fellowship, to the breaking of bread and to prayer.

ROMANS 15:4

4For everything that was written in the past was written to teach us, so that through endurance and the encouragement of the Scriptures we might have hope.

2 TIMOTHY 3:14–17

14But as for you, continue in what you have learned and have become convinced of, because you know those from whom you learned it, 15and how from infancy you have known the holy Scriptures, which are able to make you wise for salvation through faith in Christ Jesus. 16All Scripture is God-breathed and is useful for teaching, rebuking, correcting and training in righteousness, 17so that the man of God may be thoroughly equipped for every good work.

2 PETER 1:19–21

19And we have the word of the prophets made more certain, and you will do well to pay attention to it, as to a light shining in a dark place, until the day dawns and the morning star rises in your hearts. 20Above all, you must understand that no prophecy of Scripture came about by the prophet's own interpretation. 21For prophecy never had its origin in the will of man, but men spoke from God as they were carried along by the Holy Spirit.

Finding Encouragement and Endurance in the Scriptures
(Acts 2:42; Romans 15:4)

Paul's Letter to the Romans is one of the great theological letters in the New Testament. For the first eleven chapters Paul takes us to the Himalayas of New Testament theology. Then in Romans 12—16, he applied those words specifically to the lives of the believers in Rome. In Romans 14 and 15 we learn that believers with strong faith must accept those who are weak in the faith. So we believers live not for ourselves but also to build up our neighbors. Christ is our guide because he did not live to please himself. Paul quoted Psalm 69:9 to show that Jesus' followers would be insulted just as Jesus was (Rom. 15:3). Paul explained in the next verse why he used the Old Testament to teach New Testament believers: "Everything that was written in the past was written to teach us." The Scriptures are relevant to every generation of Christians because God, who inspired the Old Testament writers, had later believers in mind. How does Scripture help believers today?

Paul wrote about endurance and encouragement that bring hope. "Endurance" translates a Greek word that means *to remain under*. Through the Scriptures we find the strength to *remain under* the difficult circumstances of our lives. The Scriptures also offer us encouragement. This word comes from the same family as the word John uses to describe the Holy Spirit as a Counselor or Comforter (John 14:16, 26; 16:7). The English meaning is helpful as well because God encourages his people by putting courage in them. This gives us hope. Remember that the word *hope* speaks of a confident expectation.

Equipping God's People for Every Good Work
(2 Timothy 3:14–17)

In the final letter Paul wrote, he reminded Timothy that the same Spirit who comforts and encourages believers inspired the Scriptures. Paul, in his last letter, wanted to leave Timothy with all the equipment he would need to complete the task of making disciples of all nations.

Timothy's encounter with the Scriptures began early in life. Timothy's faith first lived in his grandmother Lois and mother Eunice (2 Tim. 1:5). He had also heard Paul's teaching (2 Tim. 3:10). Paul urged

Timothy to remain in the things he had learned and become convinced of because of the credibility of his teachers (2 Tim. 3:14). Learning from his grandmother, mother, and the Apostle Paul, Timothy could have confidence that the truth he had learned was the truth he could live every day.

I resonate with Timothy because, like him, I learned from a godly mother. My mother taught me in Vacation Bible School early in my life. When I was a teenager, I remember returning home in the evening to find her at the kitchen table reading the Scriptures. Her Bible came alive in her life and ours as she took four boys to Sunday School and church by herself. She answered my questions about salvation in the kitchen of our third floor apartment in Schrollbach, West Germany, before I prayed to receive Christ as my Savior.

What benefit could Timothy derive from the Scriptures? Paul told him the Scriptures were able to make one wise for salvation through faith in Jesus Christ. Since God breathed the Scriptures into the lives of the writers, the Scriptures offered the multiple benefits of being useful for teaching, rebuking, correcting, and training in righteousness. Sometimes God uses the Scriptures to teach and to train us positively. At other times, God uses them to rebuke and correct his people. All of these benefits of Scripture equip God's servants to accomplish every good work.

A friend of mine is a very successful businessman in our community and a Sunday School teacher in our church. He accepted my challenge to our congregation nine years ago to read through the Bible each year. During that time he has begun to preach in nursing homes and local churches while he has continued to teach his class. He says that his life and his family have been greatly enriched by this commitment to read

DISCIPLE

The word *disciple* means *one who is taught or learns*. When Jesus taught in the Great Commission that his followers were to make disciples, he never intended that his church simply make converts (Matthew 28:18–20). Not only would these new believers need to be baptized, but they would also need to be instructed in all things that Christ commanded.

God's word. Last year his son, an eighth grader, joined his father in reading through the Bible. Both have become leaders in their ministries in our church.

Acting on the Authority of Scripture (2 Peter 1:19–21)

In the Second Epistle of Peter, the writer reminded the readers that they had been established in truth from the beginning. As an eyewitness to the transfiguration, Peter recounted the Father's words to the Son, "This is my Son whom I love; with him I am well pleased" (2 Pet. 1:17). Peter connected these words with the words of the prophets in the picturesque imagery of a light dawning and the morning star rising in the hearts of his readers.

The power Peter envisioned in the Scriptures derives from the source of Scripture. Prophets did not come up with their own ideas and interpretations. In fact, prophecy did not originate with the will of human beings, but these prophets spoke from God, carried along by the Holy Spirit.

In these days when many question the idea of moral absolutes, Peter's words bring great comfort. We have a sure word from God in the Scriptures. He gave the prophets the words, speaking through their personalities, to the people of their own generation and also to ours.

As believers today, we base our decisions individually and corporately on the teachings of Scripture. In the New Testament tradition, we do not build our lives on human traditions and ideas. Neither do we find God's will through individual opinions. The priesthood of the believer means we have access to God's will as the Spirit guides us into truth. This does not mean, however, that every believer can decide for himself or herself what the Bible means. Again and again, we must return to the text and interpret it together in community.

As a pastor for the past twenty-six years, I have taken delight in the marvelous tapestry of personalities whom God has woven into the church. One of the unique men of God I have met was Dr. Ben Oliver. During the 1990s, I served as his pastor while he and his wife Edith were in their nineties. Ben was a missionary in Brazil who retired after thirty-seven years of service in 1968. When I met him in Austin, he was still reading through the New Testament every year—in Greek. We sat

> # HOW TO INTERPRET SCRIPTURE
>
> What is the right way to interpret Scripture? We should read all of Scripture in context instead of isolating individual verses to prove our personal agendas. We should also interpret the Bible in community. It is unlikely that one individual will come up with a unique interpretation that none of God's people have ever seen in the last 2,000 years. We may place great trust in God's people making sound decisions as we pray together and seek to understand Scripture together.

and translated together in his living room. He sat in his favorite recliner, which he called his *vinyl resting place.*

At Ben's graveside, a longtime friend defined Ben's life for me in three words, *intellect on fire.* His great mind and heart were set on fire by the Spirit through his deep devotion to study the Scriptures. It seemed to all of us, that like Elijah, Ben might have skipped death and been escorted out by chariots of fire from above. He left his Greek New Testament with me after his death. I use it nearly every day. At his funeral, I prayed that God would give me a double portion of his Spirit. I was reminded that I was making a hard request. From the beginning of our spiritual lives until the day God calls us home, God's word is a torch that will guide us until we arrive safely home.

Implications and Actions

Like the first church which met in Jerusalem, New Testament churches today find real help in the apostles' teachings. When we study the Scriptures and share them together, our lives are greatly strengthened. It is one thing to say that we are *people of the book.* It is another to make it a "lamp to our feet and light to our path" (Psalm 119:105). Why not commit to use a plan and read through the Bible each year? God will speak to us in his word.

QUESTIONS

1. How did Peter use the Scriptures in his sermon at Pentecost (Acts 2:14–36)? What references did he make to the Old Testament?

2. Read Paul's words in Romans 15:4. In what ways have the Scriptures given you endurance, encouragement, and hope?

3. Timothy's faith first lived in his grandmother and mother. Where did your faith first live?

4. Who were Sunday School teachers and other Christians who significantly contributed to your faith development? How did faith live in them? How does it live in you as a result of their guidance?

5. In what way does the reading of Scripture correct you or rebuke you today? How does it teach and train you in righteousness? How will you respond?

6. How do you believe the Scriptures came to us (2 Peter 1:21)? How then should we respond to God's word to us in the Scriptures?

FOCAL TEXT
Acts 2:42–47;
1 Corinthians 12:4–11;
Philippians 1:3–9

BACKGROUND
Acts 2:42–47; 4:32–37;
1 Corinthians 12:4–11;
Philippians 1:1–11

MAIN IDEA
A New Testament church
shares with one another in
genuine, deepening fellowship.

QUESTION TO EXPLORE
How can the fellowship in your
church be made stronger?

STUDY AIM
To compare the fellowship
of my church with that of
the New Testament church
and identify ways in which
my church's fellowship
can be made stronger

QUICK READ
The New Testament church
loved to be together, meet
together, and eat together,
because they shared authentic
Christian fellowship in Christ.

LESSON ELEVEN
Share Genuine Fellowship

We don't meet unless we eat! Most of my early memories of church fellowship revolved around meals—more specifically potluck suppers. At a Baptist church in Germany, we had an annual church softball game and picnic. A church composed of officers and enlisted men from the military gathered under the pine trees to eat our individual meals separately. Some came with grills and cooked steak; others brought chicken or peanut butter and jelly sandwiches. After the softball game, we would go to our own tables.

But when our new pastor came, he would have none of that. He asked some deacons to line up all the picnic tables end to end, and everybody spread out their food in a line. Thus, some who brought hot dogs ended up eating steak and vice versa. We may not remember what we ate that day, but the sweet taste of fellowship left a lasting memory of the right way for church members to share our lives together.

ACTS 2:42–47

[42]They devoted themselves to the apostles' teaching and to the fellowship, to the breaking of bread and to prayer. [43]Everyone was filled with awe, and many wonders and miraculous signs were done by the apostles. [44]All the believers were together and had everything in common. [45]Selling their possessions and goods, they gave to anyone as he had need. [46]Every day they continued to meet together in the temple courts. They broke bread in their homes and ate together with glad and sincere hearts, [47]praising God and enjoying the favor of all the people. And the Lord added to their number daily those who were being saved.

1 CORINTHIANS 12:4–11

[4]There are different kinds of gifts, but the same Spirit. [5]There are different kinds of service, but the same Lord. [6]There are different kinds of working, but the same God works all of them in all men.

[7]Now to each one the manifestation of the Spirit is given for the common good. [8]To one there is given through the Spirit the message of wisdom, to another the message of knowledge by

means of the same Spirit, [9] to another faith by the same Spirit, to another gifts of healing by that one Spirit, [10] to another miraculous powers, to another prophecy, to another distinguishing between spirits, to another speaking in different kinds of tongues, and to still another the interpretation of tongues. [11] All these are the work of one and the same Spirit, and he gives them to each one, just as he determines.

PHILIPPIANS 1:3–9

[3] I thank my God every time I remember you. [4] In all my prayers for all of you, I always pray with joy [5] because of your partnership in the gospel from the first day until now, [6] being confident of this, that he who began a good work in you will carry it on to completion until the day of Christ Jesus.

[7] It is right for me to feel this way about all of you, since I have you in my heart; for whether I am in chains or defending and confirming the gospel, all of you share in God's grace with me. [8] God can testify how I long for all of you with the affection of Christ Jesus.

[9] And this is my prayer: that your love may abound more and more in knowledge and depth of insight. . . .

Sharing God's Life Together (Acts 2:43–45)

After Peter's sermon at Pentecost, the church grew by a multiple of twenty-six, from 120 to 3,120 believers in a single day. People from different language and cultural groups came together as one church in Christ. This diverse group found unity not only in the apostles' teaching but also in a shared commitment to fellowship.

This word *koinonia* or fellowship means to share all things in common. The early church liked to be together. Three times Luke, the author of Acts, told us they were together. All the believers were together (2:44). They continued to meet together in the temple courts (2:46). They ate together with glad and sincere hearts (2:46). The early believers loved sharing life together in their homes. When we offer Christian hospitality, we open the possibility of sharing our lives in a lonely world.

In an age where we increasingly live separate lives, not knowing our neighbors, the early church reminds us of the healthiness of Christian relationships. We can be like porcupines huddling together in the cold—we want to get close to one another, but when we do it hurts.

By contrast, the disciples devoted themselves to fellowship. In this generation, many churches have chosen to place the word *fellowship* in their names. Fellowship is an essential dimension of the life of the church. Is your church a place of genuine fellowship?

Recently we received an e-mail in the general box of our church web site. The woman who wrote asked a simple question, "Is there room in your church for a lonely old sinner?" We wrote her back, and later she discovered community with us in the church.

Sharing God's Gifts Together (1 Corinthians 12:4–11)

Christians experience unity not in spite of their diversity but in their diversity. The God who lives in eternal community as the triune God (Father, Son, and Holy Spirit) created humankind in his image so that we might also celebrate community. In fact, as Paul taught the church at Corinth about the diverse gifts within the church, he reminded them that God alone could bestow the gifts and put the members of the body together as he saw fit (1 Cor. 12:4–11). God intended for the gifts to accomplish his purposes of bringing common good (12:7) and not to bring attention to the one who received the gift.

No single list of spiritual gifts in the New Testament is exhaustive. For example, New Testament writers list the gifts in several different places (1 Cor. 2:8–11; Romans 12:6–8; Ephesians 4:11; 1 Peter 4:10–11). We notice immediately the diversity of these gifts. The same Spirit apportions the gifts of wisdom and knowledge. To another the Spirit gives faith—supernatural trust in God. In the church at Corinth, we discover highly visible spectacular gifts like healing and miraculous powers. Some possess in the Spirit the gift of prophecy, which is more about speaking a relevant message for God than about predicting the future. Other believers manifest great discernment to distinguish between the

TONGUES

The gift of tongues apparently caused division and consternation in the church at Corinth. What was this gift? Ever since Pentecost when the crowd heard the gospel in their own languages, the manifestation of tongues as a gift from God has captured the attention of people (Acts 2:7–13). Some apparently elevated this gift as a superior gift to the others because of the spectacular nature of the gift. Paul placed this gift in perspective by saying that even if we speak with the tongues of human beings and angels it will not help the church unless the gift is used in love (1 Cor. 13:1–3). To this day the manifestation of tongues sometimes creates division in churches. Some answer this concern by saying the gifts belonged to the apostles and are no longer available to the church. Others argue that all of the gifts of the New Testament remain with the church today. Paul gave very specific guidelines about the gift when he wrote, "But in the church I would rather speak five intelligible words to instruct others than ten thousand words in a tongue" (1 Cor. 14:19).

spirits. Still others have the ability to speak in different kinds of tongues and to interpret those tongues.

These diverse gifts call us to live not in independence but in interdependence. The same Giver has given the gifts and placed us right where he wants us in the body of Christ. For this reason, Paul made it clear that it would be a mistake for one member of the body to say, *The church doesn't need me* (1 Cor. 12:15–18), or *I don't need the church* (1 Cor. 12:21–24). Christian fellowship means that we need each other, just as the diverse parts of the human body need one another for life.

Sharing the Gospel Together (Philippians 1:3–9)

Fellowship in the early church was more about ministry than meals. So Paul used this word *koinonia* to describe the partnership he shared in the gospel with the church at Phillipi. In this letter, Paul spoke openly and honestly about his relationship with the members of the church there.

We learn from the Book of Acts that the first members of the church in Philippi represented divergent backgrounds (Acts 16). Upon Paul's response to the Macedonian call, Paul and his companions arrived in Philippi to find a group of women who left the city on the Sabbath to pray. One of them, Lydia, insisted on hosting the apostles in her own home (Acts 16:11–15). Later a slave girl and a jailor became followers of Christ as well (Acts 16:16–34). Out of these diverse beginnings, God developed a remarkable church.

In this vignette from Paul's letter to Philippi, we see his spiritual concern for his partners who shared in the fellowship of the gospel. In Philippians 1:3–4 we learn that he prayed for them with joy because of their partnership in the gospel. The word translated "partnership" is once again *koinonia* or fellowship.

What was the basis of their sharing? They shared a common commitment to the good news of Jesus Christ. God began a good work at Philippi and was carrying it forward even as Paul wrote to the believers a letter of gratitude for their financial support of his ministry. So their partnership was inherently spiritual in nature. Too, they shared a common hope of Christ's return (Phil. 1:6). Paul wrote

HOW WE TREAT ONE ANOTHER

Years ago I served a wonderful rural church that retained its older facilities and pews from the time of the Second World War. Some members wanted to replace the wooden opera chairs with pews. Others wanted to *keep the church the same.*

Eventually, the pro-pew party won the vote in a business meeting, and we remodeled the church with beautiful new pews. Some who won gloated. Those who lost glowered and wondered whether the church would ever be the same.

As a teen-aged pastor, I stood and confidently addressed this fellowship issue: "God doesn't care whether we sit on pews, or on chairs, or even on the floor. But he does care how we treat one another." The Lord used my sincere heart and simple words to call the church back to fellowship.

Is there any issue that currently divides your congregation? Is it more important than your shared life together? How will you work to restore fellowship?

about his personal feelings for the church when he told them that they were in his heart (Phil. 1:7). Once again Paul used the word *koinonia* in describing how the Philippians share in God's grace with him (Phil. 1:7). He longed for them not just as friends commonly would, but with the "affection of Christ Jesus." We must love one another as Christ loves us.

Some years ago an American pastor tried to convince a British brother that the apostle Paul was not really much of a pastor. My British friend cited this very passage to demonstrate Paul's pastoral heart. We hear it also in Paul's prayer (Phil. 1:9–11). As remarkable as their fellowship was, Paul prayed that their love would grow more and more.

Knowledge enlightened this Christian fellowship as well. As we believers grow together in deep insight, we are able to discern what is best and become pure and blameless until Christ comes. In our lives, the Spirit will bear fruit that comes through Christ to the glory and praise of God.

Implications and Actions

Fellowship must mean more than a meal. The substance of our sharing is not determined by the menu of the meal, but by the deeper sharing of our lives. Our churches today approach the New Testament model best when we share our lives, our spiritual gifts, and a common purpose together. Through the gospel, God creates deeper friendships and partnerships in the church than any other earthly organization can imagine or create.

QUESTIONS

1. How does your church intentionally plan to share in Christian *koinonia*?

2. How have you rejoiced with those who rejoice and wept with those who weep in your church (Romans 12:15)?

3. What is your spiritual gift or gifts? How do you need the gifts of others to become complete?

4. How does Paul's relationship with the church at Philippi inform your relationship with the ministers and other members of your congregation?

5. What is the one strongest force that brings your church together?

FOCAL TEXT
Acts 2:42–47;
1 Corinthians 11:17–34;
Ephesians 5:19–20

BACKGROUND
Acts 2:42–47; 4:23–31; 20:7–12;
1 Corinthians 11:17–34; 14:26–33;
Ephesians 5:19–20;
Hebrews 10:24–25

MAIN IDEA
A New Testament church
worships the Lord together.

QUESTION TO EXPLORE
How does our church's
experience of worship compare
to that of the early church?

STUDY AIM
To identify how I can
participate in my church's
worship more effectively

QUICK READ
As a New Testament church,
we were born again to worship
God with our attitudes,
our actions, and our all.

LESSON TWELVE
Worship Together

Do you remember your favorite worship service? As a college freshman 1,600 miles from home, I found myself struggling with depression. All week long at school I had struggled with a dark, disabling gloom. When Sunday came, I went to church even though I did not feel like going. As I entered the foyer, I heard the choir beginning the call to worship. Somehow as they sang about God's love lifting us, their words became my reality. The darkness lifted, and light poured into my soul as the reality of God's presence comforted and encouraged me. A friend in the choir said she saw the change in my countenance as the congregation began to sing in response to the call to worship.

In our consumer age, discussions of worship often become monologues as Christians seek to convince others to accept their worship preference while failing to listen to those with differing ideas. People shop for churches in which their particular worship preferences prevail. But, what if real worship is not about getting what we want, but about God getting what he wants in our lives?

ACTS 2:42–47

[42]They devoted themselves to the apostles' teaching and to the fellowship, to the breaking of bread and to prayer. [43]Everyone was filled with awe, and many wonders and miraculous signs were done by the apostles. [44]All the believers were together and had everything in common. [45]Selling their possessions and goods, they gave to anyone as he had need. [46]Every day they continued to meet together in the temple courts. They broke bread in their homes and ate together with glad and sincere hearts, [47]praising God and enjoying the favor of all the people. And the Lord added to their number daily those who were being saved.

1 CORINTHIANS 11:17–34

[17]In the following directives I have no praise for you, for your meetings do more harm than good. [18]In the first place, I hear that when you come together as a church, there are divisions among you, and to some extent I believe it. [19]No doubt there have to be

differences among you to show which of you have God's approval. [20]When you come together, it is not the Lord's Supper you eat, [21]for as you eat, each of you goes ahead without waiting for anybody else. One remains hungry, another gets drunk. [22]Don't you have homes to eat and drink in? Or do you despise the church of God and humiliate those who have nothing? What shall I say to you? Shall I praise you for this? Certainly not!

[23]For I received from the Lord what I also passed on to you: The Lord Jesus, on the night he was betrayed, took bread, [24]and when he had given thanks, he broke it and said, "This is my body, which is for you; do this in remembrance of me." [25]In the same way, after supper he took the cup, saying, "This cup is the new covenant in my blood; do this, whenever you drink it, in remembrance of me." [26]For whenever you eat this bread and drink this cup, you proclaim the Lord's death until he comes.

[27]Therefore, whoever eats the bread or drinks the cup of the Lord in an unworthy manner will be guilty of sinning against the body and blood of the Lord. [28]A man ought to examine himself before he eats of the bread and drinks of the cup. [29]For anyone who eats and drinks without recognizing the body of the Lord eats and drinks judgment on himself. [30]That is why many among you are weak and sick, and a number of you have fallen asleep. [31]But if we judged ourselves, we would not come under judgment. [32]When we are judged by the Lord, we are being disciplined so that we will not be condemned with the world.

[33]So then, my brothers, when you come together to eat, wait for each other. [34]If anyone is hungry, he should eat at home, so that when you meet together it may not result in judgment.

And when I come I will give further directions.

EPHESIANS 5:19–20

[19]Speak to one another with psalms, hymns and spiritual songs. Sing and make music in your heart to the Lord, [20]always giving thanks to God the Father for everything, in the name of our Lord Jesus Christ.

Consumed In Worship (Acts 2:42–47)

The early believers were not consumers of worship; they were consumed in worship. Luke used the word "devoted" to describe this commitment (Acts 2:42). They were strongly "devoted" to the apostles' teaching, to fellowship, to the breaking of bread, and to the prayers.

The early church loved to fulfill Christ's commandment of breaking bread together in the Lord's Supper. The disciples broke bread from house to house (Acts 2:46) and also committed themselves to prayer. Although the NIV translates this simply as "prayer," a better rendering is *the prayers*. What role does prayer play in your corporate worship? The worship leader at our church sets aside a season of silence in our worship and calls it *the prayers of the people*. This silence may make us uncomfortable initially, but it evokes a deep sense of dependence and trust as we find God speaking to us in the silence. Corporate prayer empowers the church for our mission in the world. At prayer, the apostles encountered a lame man as Peter and John went up to the temple at the regular hour of the afternoon prayer (Acts 3:1–8).

The believers in Jerusalem coupled their devotion with a deep sense of awe over God's work among them through the wonders and signs performed by the apostles (Acts 2:43). This sense of fear or reverence is often set aside in churches today as some Christians redefine worship exclusively in terms of celebration. To the contrary, sometimes worship is confrontation, coming like Isaiah face to face with God's holiness and recognizing our own sin (Isaiah 6:1–8). This awe also speaks of the worshipers' sense of anticipation. The people were devoted to worship because they expected God to do something great among them. We ask our people to come to worship expecting God to do something so great that God alone can take credit for it.

The disciples also experienced gladness and offered praise to God in worship (Acts 2:46–47). These verses show the early church in powerful celebration. Years ago I worshiped with a church in Brazil where the joyful countenances of God's people overflowed in praise to God as they sang "Jesus Satisfies." God is delighted in us when we are satisfied with him. This means we worship not only with our mind's attention but also with our heart's affection.

I heard of one Christian who was criticized by another as being *too happy*. Yet, this very gladness made the early church winsome to the

WORSHIPING IN A DIFFERENT WAY

Recently our church's Burmese congregation celebrated their second anniversary. First, we sang a familiar hymn in English. Later I watched with awe and joy as they sang a chorus in their own language. I couldn't sing the song, but I worshiped anyway—I was soaking it up watching them sing for joy to our God who knows no linguistic limitations.

community around them. They enjoyed the favor of others precisely because they were constantly and authentically offering praise to God. Although worship does not uniquely consist in praise, God-centered worship leads believers to talk about God everywhere we go even as newlyweds love to talk about their spouses.

While Christian worship includes both confrontation and celebration, the New Testament does not specifically prescribe activities and orders of service as normative. Different churches have worshiped in different ways at different times.

Communion in Worship (1 Corinthians 11:17–34)

People ask many questions these days about the Lord's Supper, such as, *How often should we partake of the Lord's Supper?* Different denominational traditions and various churches observe this ordinance with differing frequency.

As the church expanded, the Apostle Paul established a church in Corinth and remained there for eighteen months (Acts 18:11). Later he wrote to the church as it struggled to survive and grow in a pagan city. Because Paul's letters likely preceded the gospels, Paul offered the first New Testament description of this ordinance. In his description of the Lord's Supper, Paul gave particular instructions because the church's approach was doing more harm than good (1 Cor. 11:17). Divisions within the church and impatience in eating before others arrived disrupted worship and fellowship (1 Cor. 11:18–22). Often the Lord's Supper was preceded by or even consisted of a *love feast* or a larger meal.

Consider what the Lord's Supper does for us and how we should respond. First, the Lord's Supper offers us fellowship with the crucified and risen Lord. Paul maintained that the risen Lord was the one who gave him these teachings about the Lord's Supper (1 Cor. 11:23). Too, the Lord's Supper allows the church to focus on Christ, to proclaim Christ's death, and to anticipate his return (1 Cor. 11:23–27). Further, the Lord's Supper calls for spiritual preparation. Paul invited believers to examine themselves before eating and drinking, recognizing the sacredness of the supper as a remembrance of Christ's death. Failure to do so would constitute sin against the body and blood of the Lord. Today, we do not come lightly to the Lord's table as though it were a trivial ritual.

Sometimes we struggle to communicate what it means to eat the Lord's Supper in a worthy manner (1 Cor. 11:27). One friend at a student pastorate tried to convey the reverent examination necessary to come to the table but unintentionally convinced the people not to partake at all! In a service in England on a recent sabbatical, I heard a minister catch the spirit of eating the Lord's Supper in a worthy manner. He said that we do not presume to come to the Lord's table in our own goodness because we are not worthy even to receive the crumbs that fall from the table. Later he joyfully showed us that we come in the worthiness of the Christ who shed his blood for all of our sins. The Lord's Supper is not for sinless people but for sinners who are grateful for God's grace.

The Lord's Supper also offers us fellowship with one another. Paul first addressed the Corinthians as members of the same family, as brothers and sisters (1 Cor. 11:33). Paul concluded by telling the people to wait for one another and to eat their meals at home if they were hungry (1 Cor. 11:34).

Christ died to reconcile humankind to God and to each other. What a shame it would be if divisions in worship overshadowed the memory of what Christ did to unite people with himself. When we observe the Lord's Supper, we must care about the needs of others as well as our own needs.

Communicating Our Worship (Ephesians 5:19–20)

Most discussions of worship these days devolve to arguments about musical styles. Some Christians favor quiet and reverent music while others prefer the majestic notes played on an organ. Still others use guitars, drums, and keyboards.

Instrumental preference is not a biblical issue since most of these instruments did not exist in their current forms in the first century. In fact, the psalmist called for the use of a great variety of instruments to express worship (Psalm 150:3–5). However, the ways we relate to each other in our discussions about worship are deeply biblical and spiritual issues.

What does the New Testament teach us about music in the church? In his letter to the Ephesians, Paul portrayed Christians as a singing people who communicated with one another through psalms, hymns, and spiritual songs (Eph. 5:19). Even in the first-century church, worship included different types of songs. Like the Israelites before them, the early Christians sang the psalms. The believers also wrote hymns and sang new songs inspired by the Spirit.

Christian worship is not confined to a service or a time of the week. Christians worship through songs not only in the service, but everywhere we go. Paul urged that believers should make music in their hearts to the Lord (Eph. 5:19).

More important than the style of music is the attitude of thankfulness to God the Father in the name of the Lord Jesus Christ. Christian worship rooted in the doctrine of the Trinity expresses a recognition of the triune God as we sing in the Spirit to the Father in the authority or power of Jesus Christ. Worship is about God and about strengthening the church with our songs and our sermons (1 Cor. 14:26–32).

DIFFERING VIEWS ON THE LORD'S SUPPER

Some traditions teach that the bread and the cup of the Lord's Supper are literally transformed into the body and blood of Christ. Another view is that the elements incorporate Christ's presence within them without a literal transformation of the elements. Baptists see the Lord's Supper as more of a memorial meal.

We must be careful not to say that the Lord's Supper is *just a symbol*, though. Symbols possess power because of what they represent. Christ's body and blood represent the eternal life Christ died to provide.

Early Christians preached and listened to sermons in worship (Acts 20:7). Paul's lengthy sermon was one of the first to put a listener to sleep, as Eutychus fell from the window after dozing off. After Paul and the others realized he was still alive, Paul preached the rest of the night (Acts 20:8–11). In some services, more than one preacher preached (1 Cor. 14:29–31). Paul sought to add a sense of order and propriety to these spontaneous services of worship. The God of peace takes no delight in disorder (1 Cor. 14:33). Today as then, whether we worship with complex liturgical order or in a more spontaneous fashion, our primary concern must be for mutual encouragement and strengthening of each other (1 Cor. 14:26, 31).

Commitment to Worship (Hebrews 10:24–25)

Prior to these verses in Hebrews, the writer has offered a long theological discussion about Christ's preeminence over angels and Moses. The writer also showed how Jesus fulfilled the Old Testament teachings about worship and sacrifice through his once and for all death on the cross (Heb. 10:12). Four times in a row the writer urged the believers to community in worship with the expression, "Let us . . ." (Heb. 10:22–25). Believers worship best in community, not in isolation.

Why do we need to meet together? The writer of Hebrews taught that worship is not primarily about our own personal preferences and individual spiritual growth. These days we can certainly hear great sermons and worship music on television and on the computer. But good sermons do not substitute for mutual encouragement. Discipleship happens in community with other believers. Together we find the acceptance and accountability we need to grow as Christians.

As we worship in community, we take thought of each other's needs so that we may spur one another on to good deeds. Some in the first century no longer met together regularly. But the writer of Hebrews corrected this behavior. Believers encourage each other especially because we "see the Day approaching."

The Day of the Lord was a description the prophets used to predict the climactic moment in history when God's judgment would take place (Joel 2:31; Malachi 3:1–2). Early Christians understood this day as the day of Christ's return.

When we gather together, we have the chance to encourage each other in anticipation of the great consummation of the ages when Christ returns personally, visibly, powerfully, and victoriously. No matter what day of the week Christ returns, may his followers be found in a perpetual state of worship, expressing our love to him in our attitudes and actions.

Implications and Actions

The New Testament corrects selfishness in worship. In our celebration of the Lord's Supper—our prayers, our music, and our teaching—we must offer honor to God first as we take thought of the needs of God's people.

In the *worship wars* of our day, elements of worship that should draw attention to God are often used as weapons to prove our own personal preferences. We may know what we like and like what we know about music and preaching, but true worship calls us to know the Lord.

For this reason, we do not go to worship to evaluate others but to be evaluated by God. Because God is the only audience for our worship, the right questions for the worshiper to ask are, *How did I do today, Lord? Did I give you my best attitudes and actions?*

QUESTIONS

1. What role does prayer play in your worship services?

2. Do you remember feeling a deep sense of awe in worship?

3. How do you personally prepare for the Lord's Supper?

4. What are some appropriate ways to sing or to preach in worship?

5. Can we differentiate between the biblical and cultural dimensions of our worship preferences? For instance, does the Bible prescribe a particular musical style or liturgical order? Should believers divide over cultural preferences?

FOCAL TEXT
Acts 2:43–45; 3:1–8;
1 Corinthians 16:1–3;
James 2:14–17

BACKGROUND
Acts 2:42–47; 3:1–10;
1 Corinthians 16:1–3;
James 2:14–17

MAIN IDEA
A New Testament church
ministers to people's needs.

QUESTION TO EXPLORE
In what ways do you and
your church minister
to people's needs?

STUDY AIM
To identify ways I will join
my church in ministering
to people's needs

QUICK READ
Real ministry that is rooted
in love cannot be confined
within the walls of the church.
In a New Testament church,
members start out taking
care of one another but end
up caring for the world.

LESSON THIRTEEN
Minister to People's Needs

Many years ago, our small church outside of Waco, Texas, became aware of a need in the Billington community. Down a dirt road lay a series of homes with many children who did not go to church. Our church, Williams Creek Baptist Church, bought a used van to pick up the children for our services. Over the years, this van opened up the opportunity for ministry to many physical needs as we cared for these families. One Christmas morning we delivered presents to a family who had no way to buy gifts. Many of those children gave their lives to Christ because of the church's concern. The ministry cost our members many hours of time but offered a fruitful opportunity for ministry and evangelism.

What should the church do about the enormous physical need in our world? Newspapers could report thousands of deaths every day because of extreme poverty. Every day many children in our world die of malaria, while many adults die of tuberculosis. Many young adults die of AIDS every day. The enormity of the need can be mind-numbing. We are tempted to wring our hands and say, *Look what the world has come to.* Or worse yet to say, *Whew, I'm glad I'm not having those problems.* How do we overcome our compassion fatigue—that paralysis that asks, *What can we do in a world with such great need?*

The New Testament church responded to physical needs with unwavering compassion. Who told the church that its job was to care for the needs of others? Early Christians had seen Jesus look at the hungry multitude of five thousand with compassion and tell his disciples to feed them (Luke 9:13). The early church did not succumb to compassion fatigue.

These Christians did what they could. The apostles were busy performing miraculous signs and wonders like healing the crippled beggar (Acts 3:1–10). At the same time, the disciples did what they could by selling their possessions and goods and giving to anyone who had a need. Luke later described the church: "There were no needy persons among them. For from time to time those who owned lands or houses sold them, brought the money from the sales and put it at the apostles' feet, and it was distributed to anyone as he had need" (Acts 4:34–35). When some of the Grecian widows felt neglected, the apostles said, "It would not be right for us to neglect the ministry of the word of God to wait on tables" (Acts 6:2). Because the needs had to be addressed, the church installed lay leaders as servants to provide for the needs (Acts 6:1–7). This act shows us that the church's ministry is both social and spiritual. For this reason, we combine our caring acts with thoughtful teaching of the truth.

The church serves by helping the people inside the church as well as those outside the church. Meeting needs always entails a cost. Sometimes it costs us financially. At other times it costs us time. But if we took what God has given us and cared for souls both inside and outside the church, we would be able to meet the needs of many people. Real ministry, rooted in love, cannot be confined within the walls of the church. We start out taking care of one another, but we end up caring for the world.

ACTS 2:43–45

⁴³Everyone was filled with awe, and many wonders and miraculous signs were done by the apostles. ⁴⁴All the believers were together and had everything in common. ⁴⁵Selling their possessions and goods, they gave to anyone as he had need.

ACTS 3:1–8

¹One day Peter and John were going up to the temple at the time of prayer—at three in the afternoon. ²Now a man crippled from birth was being carried to the temple gate called Beautiful, where he was put every day to beg from those going into the temple courts. ³When he saw Peter and John about to enter, he asked them for money. ⁴Peter looked straight at him, as did John. Then Peter said, "Look at us!" ⁵So the man gave them his attention, expecting to get something from them.

⁶Then Peter said, "Silver or gold I do not have, but what I have I give you. In the name of Jesus Christ of Nazareth, walk." ⁷Taking him by the right hand, he helped him up, and instantly the man's feet and ankles became strong. ⁸He jumped to his feet and began to walk. Then he went with them into the temple courts, walking and jumping, and praising God.

1 CORINTHIANS 16:1–3

[1]Now about the collection for God's people: Do what I told the Galatian churches to do. [2]On the first day of every week, each one of you should set aside a sum of money in keeping with his income, saving it up, so that when I come no collections will have to be made. [3]Then, when I arrive, I will give letters of introduction to the men you approve and send them with your gift to Jerusalem.

JAMES 2:14–17

[14]What good is it, my brothers, if a man claims to have faith but has no deeds? Can such faith save him? [15]Suppose a brother or sister is without clothes and daily food. [16]If one of you says to him, "Go, I wish you well; keep warm and well fed," but does nothing about his physical needs, what good is it? [17]In the same way, faith by itself, if it is not accompanied by action, is dead.

Meeting Needs Inside the Body
(Acts 2:43–45; 4:34–36; 1 Corinthians 16:1–3; James 2:14–17)

How do we meet needs within the church? First, we have to be willing to sacrifice and divest ourselves of what God has given to us. A true Christian cannot stand to have too much while others do not have enough. We notice in the church at Jerusalem that all the believers were together and had everything in common (Acts 2:43–45). They sold their possessions and goods in order to share with others. When Joseph, also called Barnabas, sold a field and laid the proceeds at the apostles' feet, they called him "Son of Encouragement" (Acts 4:36–37).

One friend of mine was a multimillionaire, but he never bought a new suit in the last twenty years of his life. His automobiles were not extravagant. He had learned to live simply so that he could give generously to meet the needs of others.

In our affluent society we must constantly ask ourselves whether our possessions have become too important to us. Some Christians wonder, *Are we too wealthy for God to use us? Do we cling to our possessions to our own detriment?* Everything we have comes from the Lord. The early believers were willing to surrender their possessions because they understood the psalmist's words, "The earth is the Lord's and everything in it, the world and all who live in it" (Psalms 24:1).

Second, we must learn to share what we have with others. So the early Christians gave as anyone had need (Acts 2:45). God promised the ancient Israelites that among the people of God there should be no unmet needs (Deuteronomy 15:4). This promise came true in the church (Acts 4:34).

When the Jerusalem church later suffered from severe financial deprivation, Paul urged the believers in Corinth to participate in an offering for "God's people" (1 Cor. 16:1). These Gentile believers practiced these same principles of sacrifice in order to share with others. We notice that their giving was to be regular, "On the first day of every week" (1 Cor. 16:2). All the members participated in the offering (1 Cor. 16:2). Paul commended proportional giving as each shared, "in keeping with his income" (1 Cor. 16:2). So the Corinthian believers were to join the Galatian believers in preparing to give even before Paul arrived to collect the offering for the church in Jerusalem. The New Testament church teaches us that sharing our lives involves putting our Christianity into action.

Christian compassion calls on the church to identify the real needs inside the body of Christ. Later James showed the first-century believers that real faith demonstrates compassion through works. When they saw brothers or sisters without clothes or daily food, they had to offer

PRACTICAL MINISTRY

Think of practical ways your church can minister to the physical needs of people in your community. Some churches have offered free car washes and told the beneficiaries, *We do not want to raise money but to show you the love of Christ in a tangible way.* Other churches have gone to laundromats with quarters and detergent, offering them to people to show the love of Christ. Many communities have food and clothing banks for churches to support to meet needs. We cannot do everything, but we can do something. By God's grace, let us do what we can.

more than words and empty sentiment. To demonstrate the reality of our faith, we believers must do good to one another and respond to one another's needs tangibly (James 2:14–17).

After we care for members within the body of Christ, what responsibility do we have towards unbelievers? Once love fills the house, it overflows into the streets.

Meeting Needs Outside the Body (Acts 2:43; 3:1–8)

The apostles worked signs and wonders, not only for the believers but also for the others in the community (Acts 3:1–10). Thus the church took God's power outside the walls of the church, literally to the gates outside the temple.

The believers prepared for ministry by participating in the seasons of prayer at the temple. So Peter and John went up to the temple for the time of prayer at three o'clock in the afternoon. This was the hour of the evening sacrifice, when the people came together to watch and pray. What is the hour of prayer in our churches? Until we church members find ourselves communing with God like the apostles, we will be unprepared to meet the needs in our world. If we do not talk to God regularly, we will not be able to come to terms with the suffering we will see in the world.

When the beggar asked for help, the apostles noticed him and took time to talk to him (Acts 3:4, 6). Sometimes we church members are more like the priest and Levite in Jesus' story of the Good Samaritan (Luke 10:25–37). They were so busy for God that they took no time to care for people. Our work for God never excuses us from caring for people.

Peter and John had no silver or gold to offer to the man who begged, but they had the name of Jesus Christ and the power to heal. Most churches in the United States today can no longer say, "Silver and gold I do not have" (Acts 3:6). Compared to the truly poor in our world, we are opulently wealthy. Are we good stewards of our resources in a world where millions of children are orphans in Africa because of the AIDS epidemic?

Like Peter and John, believers today have more than money to give (Acts 3:6.) After the apostles talked to the lame man, they lifted him to his feet and offered him healing in Jesus' name (Acts 3:7). In our lonely world we must never underestimate the power of human touch. There is great dignity in a touch. As the apostles spoke encouraging words, they reached down and lifted the man to his feet and to health.

God's power transformed the man so completely that he became known as the one who previously used to beg (Acts 3:10). The love of Christians and the healing power of God lifted him from a life of poverty to a life of praise. What if believers today used our resources to offer not only physical but spiritual help to the world?

Our church recently chose an important project for our Vacation Bible School. In conjunction with our ministry through a Sudanese mission church on our campus, children learned about the needs in Sudan. Then on family night we had a Sportsathon, a gathering in which VBS students threw baseballs and footballs, shot baskets, and kicked soccer balls in order to raise money for the Sudanese people. Adult Sunday School classes pledged money to pay for each throw, shot, and kick, with all the money going to aid the people in Sudan. Our hope was that through God's power the Sudan would be transformed so that some day it might be known as the place where there *used to be* genocide and starvation.

Implications and Actions

The good news of Jesus Christ means more than merely a social gospel, but it certainly includes it. Caring for the physical needs of people will demonstrate the reality of Christ's power to meet their spiritual needs as well. When Christians respond to physical needs, we are continuing Christ's ministry to the last, lost, and least during his time on earth.

QUESTIONS

1. How is your church responding to physical needs in your community and in the world?

2. Are you ever paralyzed by the greatness of need in our world?
   How does our study of the New Testament church inform our
   fears and feelings of despair?

3. Who are the people who sit outside the doors of your church?
   How can you help them to find their way in?

4. Peter and John watched Jesus heal the sick and feed the poor.
   Does our relationship with Christ change the way we perceive and
   respond to the needs in our world?

5. How does Paul's teaching in 1 Corinthians 16:1–4 speak to our
   need to cooperate with other churches? Was there a time when
   your church received help from other churches?

6. James taught about the relationship of faith and works. How do
   our works of feeding and clothing others confirm the reality of
   our faith?

FOCAL TEXT
Acts 2:47*b*; Matthew 28:18–20;
John 20:19–21; Acts 11:19–26

BACKGROUND
Acts 2:42–47;
Matthew 28:18–20;
John 20:19–21; Acts 11:19–26

MAIN IDEA
A New Testament church
seeks to witness to all
people about Christ.

QUESTION TO EXPLORE
How important is sharing
the gospel with all the world
to you and your church?

STUDY AIM
To identify steps I will take
to witness about Christ

QUICK READ
As New Testament Christians,
we live winsome lives of
witness in obedience to
Christ's command so that
we may reach all people
with the gospel. Because of
increased transportation
and communication, our
generation has perhaps
the greatest opportunity
of any in history to obey
the Great Commission.

LESSON FOURTEEN
Witness to the World

One church has a tradition at their baptismal services of inviting the people who have influenced the new converts to receive Christ to stand during the immersion. One woman stood again and again during one service. Afterward, the pastor asked the new believers, "How did this woman influence all of you to become Christians? Did she use tracts? Was she aggressive with her witness?"

The new Christians smiled and said, "No. But she works in our office. Over time she helped all of us with our jobs. When we felt indebted to her, we asked, 'How can we pay you back for what you have done?' She said, 'Come to church with me this weekend.'"

All these coworkers had come to church, heard the gospel, and received Christ. But first, they saw her witness to the gospel as she served them in the office.

New Testament evangelism begins with relationships. As we live winsome lives, others may want to know the Christ who has changed our lives.

ACTS 2:47B

And the Lord added to their number daily those who were being saved.

MATTHEW 28:18–20

18Then Jesus came to them and said, "All authority in heaven and on earth has been given to me. 19Therefore go and make disciples of all nations, baptizing them in the name of the Father and of the Son and of the Holy Spirit, 20and teaching them to obey everything I have commanded you. And surely I am with you always, to the very end of the age."

JOHN 20:19–21

19On the evening of that first day of the week, when the disciples were together, with the doors locked for fear of the Jews, Jesus came and stood among them and said, "Peace be with you!" ²⁰After he said this, he showed them his hands and side. The disciples were overjoyed when they saw the Lord.

²¹Again Jesus said, "Peace be with you! As the Father has sent me, I am sending you."

ACTS 11:19–26

¹⁹Now those who had been scattered by the persecution in connection with Stephen traveled as far as Phoenicia, Cyprus and Antioch, telling the message only to Jews. ²⁰Some of them, however, men from Cyprus and Cyrene, went to Antioch and began to speak to Greeks also, telling them the good news about the Lord Jesus. ²¹The Lord's hand was with them, and a great number of people believed and turned to the Lord.

²²News of this reached the ears of the church at Jerusalem, and they sent Barnabas to Antioch. ²³When he arrived and saw the evidence of the grace of God, he was glad and encouraged them all to remain true to the Lord with all their hearts. ²⁴He was a good man, full of the Holy Spirit and faith, and a great number of people were brought to the Lord.

²⁵Then Barnabas went to Tarsus to look for Saul, ²⁶and when he found him, he brought him to Antioch. So for a whole year Barnabas and Saul met with the church and taught great numbers of people. The disciples were called Christians first at Antioch.

Evangelism Begins with Relationships (Acts 2:46–47)

What does New Testament evangelism look like? Luke described it simply, "The Lord added to their number those who were being saved" (Acts 2:47). Taken at face value, this statement may appear to suggest that God saved the people independently of the church's life and ministry. In fact, though, this verse comes as the crescendo of Luke's description of the life of the early church. The community around the early Christians had noticed these believers who had committed themselves to instruction in the Scriptures, to worship, to fellowship, and to ministry.

Specifically, we learn that the early Christians' gladness, sincerity, and enthusiastic love for God contributed to a likeability that captured the hearts of the unbelievers in the community (Acts 2:46–47). So evangelism is the by-product of our discipleship, worship, and fellowship.

Are we as believers characterized by gladness? What about our sincerity? We Christians hurt our own witness by saying one thing and living another. Are we caught in the adoration of God in our daily lives? As the nonbelievers in our community see the authenticity of our spiritual lives and the genuine love we have for Christ, they may be drawn to him.

A group from our church recently went to China on a trip. A Chinese national named Grace served as their guide. She explained that her name was like the song "Amazing Grace" and sang a few bars of it to the group. They learned that her grandmother had been a Christian before the expulsion of Christian missionaries during the Cultural Revolution. Grace had not made a personal commitment to Christ, however.

During the week, one of the families from our church received the bad news that one of their grandchildren had died. They chose to return to the United States to minister to their children. Before they left, the other members of the tour surrounded them and embraced them and wept with them.

Grace asked the members of the tour if they were family members of the couple who were leaving. The leaders from our church explained that they were not relatives but fellow Christians. Grace exclaimed, "I have never seen anybody love like this."

Later other members of the group had the opportunity to share the gospel with her, explaining the plan of salvation. They continue to correspond with her, praying that she will respond to Christ.

Evangelism Calls for Our Obedience to Reach Out to the World (Matthew 28:18–20; John 20:19–21)

Why did the New Testament church evangelize? The Gospel writers show us that evangelism came as a response to Christ's command to the church at the end of his earthly ministry. As Jesus was preparing to depart from his disciples, he commanded them to make disciples of all nations, baptizing and teaching them.

The Gospel of Matthew tells us often that Jesus ministered with *great authority* (Matt. 7:28–29; 8:9; 9:8). At the end of his ministry, Jesus acknowledged the great power available to his church for the work of witnessing to the world: "All authority in heaven and earth has been given to me. Therefore go" (Matt. 28:18).

Jesus also gave the church a *great purpose* when he said, "Make disciples." Jesus never told the church to make converts.

Because some doubted (Matt. 28:17), Jesus made this *great promise*, "And surely I am with you always, to the very end of the age" (Matt. 28:20). We call this passage the Great Commission because it was never a mere suggestion.

Christ's power and presence strengthened the church to accomplish its purpose of making disciples. In spite of all the growth of Christianity in our world, this commandment has not been completely fulfilled. Whole segments of our world have no current opportunity to hear the gospel. We can not outsource missions. Evangelism remains our responsibility.

The Gospel of John contains a similar challenge to the church to be missional. After his resurrection and after he had appeared to Mary Magdalene in the garden (John 20:1–18), Jesus appeared to his other disciples and offered them peace. Revealing the wounds in his hands

EVANGELIZING PEOPLE OF OTHER RELIGIONS

What about evangelizing members of other religions? Some believers practice what we might call a functional universalism. That is, they assume that all who are sincere within the diverse religions of the world are simply taking another road to a relationship with the same God as Christians.

The New Testament teachings about Christ rule out this approach as an effective strategy for evangelism. Jesus Christ is the way, the truth, and the life (John 14:6). No one comes to the Father except through him. Christians are called to engage all people with the love of Christ in authentic relationships. Recently a young missionary and member of our staff taught a course on ministry to Islamic people to increase our understanding because of the opportunity we have to share our faith in our city.

and side, Jesus again blessed them with peace. But this peace was not intended for that small group of followers alone. They took this peace with them when they accepted his commission, "As the Father has sent me, I am sending you" (John 20:21).

We sometimes confuse this teaching as one to be fulfilled by vocational missionaries. In truth, every Christian has been sent on a mission. To fulfill this commandment, we must do more than send missionaries or even go on occasional mission projects or trips. We have challenged every member of our church to see themselves on a short-term mission trip for the rest of their lives.

One of our students asked after a recent mission trip in which he had success sharing his faith and leading others to Christ, "Why is it easier to share our faith in a different city than at home?" We can not compartmentalize our commitment to evangelism. One translation of Matthew 28:18 is, *As you go, make disciples.* What if we made disciples everywhere we went? As we go, Christians live missional lives, sharing Christ in our homes, workplaces, schools, and neighborhoods.

Evangelism Explodes Barriers, Welcoming All into Relationship with Christ (Acts 11:19–26)

Whom should believers evangelize? Evangelism grew in the New Testament church in ever-increasing concentric circles. After Pentecost, the disciples shared Christ throughout Jerusalem. As they addressed fellowship issues in the church, the Lord gave them the opportunity to grow rapidly and even to reach the priests who became obedient to the faith (Acts 6:7).

After Stephen's martyrdom under the watchful eye of Saul, many in the church were forced out of Jerusalem (Acts 8:1). They fulfilled the Great Commission as they went.

Philip took the gospel to the Samaritans, who believed in great numbers (Acts 8:4–12). In obedience to God's direction through an angel, Philip left ministering to the multitudes to care for the spiritual needs of an Ethiopian eunuch traveling alone along a desert road (Acts 8:26–40). Peter shared the gospel with a God-fearing centurion (Acts 10:1–11:18).

To this point, however, the church as a whole had not invited Gentiles to become Christians. This changed at Antioch when dispersed

GOD'S SOVEREIGNTY AND OUR RESPONSIBILITY IN EVANGELISM

How do we reconcile the sovereignty of God with our responsibility in evangelism? If the "Lord added to their number those who were being saved" (Acts 2:47), isn't salvation ultimately God's work? We later read that the Lord's hand was with the church and so people were saved (Acts 11:21).

It is true that the work of salvation is God's work from beginning to end. Unless God's Spirit brings conviction and conversion, no one will be saved.

This same sovereign God, though, chooses to involve us in the work of salvation by calling us to witness to the world. As we live winsome lives in authentic relationships with God and others, God uses us to bring them into relationship with himself. The Lord's hand is with those who are obedient to his commandment to make disciples of all nations.

believers from Cyprus and Cyrene began to speak the good news about the Lord Jesus to the Greeks (Acts 11:19–20). God was with them, and for the first time, a great number of Gentiles believed and turned to the Lord (Acts 11:21).

Barnabas, dispatched by the apostles, came to Antioch, confirmed the conversion of Gentiles, and continued the work of evangelism (Acts 11:22–24). Finding Saul (Paul), who had been converted on the road to Damascus, Barnabas brought him to Antioch where they worked together to disciple these new converts (Acts 11:25–26). There the people began to call disciples Christians for the first time (Acts 11:26).

These anonymous evangelists in Antioch who witnessed to Gentiles opened a new vista for the church. Christ was no longer seen as the Savior of only the Jewish people who believed, but also of all people. This inclusiveness became contagious as the new church in Antioch sent Paul and Barnabas out on the first missionary journey to take the gospel to even more distant regions and peoples (Acts 13:1–4).

The Book of Acts confirms that sincere mission work has the opportunity of changing the lives of all who receive Christ. We have the *greatest power* in the world to accomplish the *greatest purpose* in the world with the *greatest promise* in the world. God is with us as we witness to the world.

One of the best evangelists I have ever known was a contagious witness for Christ everywhere he went. He scheduled his out-of-town business trips to synchronize with the visitation programs of churches in the towns he visited. His deep compassion for people and his passion for sharing the faith made him very effective at loving people into the kingdom of God.

Implications and Actions

New Testament Christians evangelize every day, everywhere we go, sharing with everyone we meet in everything we do. Like the early believers, we share our faith day by day. As we go, we love all people and live the gospel in front of them so that they will want to know the Christ who has transformed us.

QUESTIONS

1. In view of Acts 2:46–47 and the daily commitment of the disciples and the daily salvation of new believers, when should we as Christians witness?

2. How did the early Christians gain the favor of the people around them? How do we?

3. Do you cultivate relationships with unbelievers? Do you know your neighbors' names and needs? In what ways can you improve how you build relationships?

4. If your church takes mission trips, have you ever taken advantage of them?

5. What if you considered yourself commissioned to share Christ every day *as you go* with everyone in everything you do?

6. Is there any person or group whom you imagine to be beyond God's love and grace? How can we intentionally reach out to the people who are difficult to reach?

7. God promises to be with his people always as we make disciples. How does the promise of God's presence empower us to share our faith with others?

Our Next New Study

(Available for use beginning September 2008)

EPHESIANS, PHILIPPIANS, COLOSSIANS:
Living with Faithfulness and Joy

Additional Resources for Studying Living with Faithfulness and Joy:
Ephesians, Philippians, Colossians:[1]

EPHESIANS

Craig S. Keener. *IVP Bible Background Commentary: New Testament.*
Downers Grove, Illinois: InterVarsity Press, 1993.

Andrew T. Lincoln. *Ephesians.* Word Biblical Commentary. Volume
42. Dallas, Texas: Word Books, Publisher, 1990.

Ralph P. Martin. "Ephesians." *The Broadman Bible Commentary.*
Volume 11. Nashville, Tennessee: Broadman Press, 1971.

Pheme Perkins. "The Letter to the Ephesians." *The New Interpreter's
Bible.* Volume XI. Nashville, Tennessee: Abingdon Press, 2000.

A. T. Robertson. *Word Pictures in the New Testament.* Volume IV.
Nashville, Tennessee: Broadman Press, 1931.

PHILIPPIANS

Fred B. Craddock. *Philippians.* Interpretation: A Bible Commentary
for Teaching and Preaching. Atlanta: John Knox Press, 1985.

Morna D. Hooker. "The Letter to the Philippians." *The New
Interpreter's Bible.* Volume XI. Nashville, Tennessee: Abingdon
Press, 2000.

Ralph P. Martin. *Philippians.* Revised edition. The Tyndale New
Testament Commentaries. Grand Rapids, Michigan: William B.
Eerdmans Publishing Company, 1987.

Frank Stagg. "Philippians." *The Broadman Bible Commentary.*
Volume 11. Nashville, Tennessee: Broadman Press, 1971.

COLOSSIANS

David E. Garland. *Colossians, Philemon.* The NIV Application
Commentary. Grand Rapids, Michigan: Zondervan Publishing
House, 1998.

Andrew T. Lincoln. "The Letter to the Colossians." *The New
Interpreter's Bible.* Volume XI. Nashville, Tennessee: Abingdon
Press, 2000.

R.E.O. White. "Colossians." *The Broadman Bible Commentary.*
Volume 11. Nashville, Tennessee: Broadman Press, 1971.

NOTES

1. Listing a book does not imply full agreement by the writers or BAPTISTWAY PRESS®
with all of its comments.

How to Order More Bible Study Materials

It's easy! Just fill in the following information. For additional Bible study materials, see www.baptistwaypress.org or get a complete order form of available materials by calling 1-866-249-1799 or e-mailing baptistway@bgct.org.

Title of item	Price	Quantity	Cost
This Issue:			
Growing Together in Christ—Study Guide (BWP001036)	$3.25	_____	_____
Growing Together in Christ—Large Print Study Guide (BWP001037)	$3.55	_____	_____
Growing Together in Christ—Teaching Guide (BWP001038)	$3.75	_____	_____
Additional Issues Available:			
Genesis 12—50: Family Matters—Study Guide (BWP000034)	$1.95	_____	_____
Genesis 12—50: Family Matters—Large Print Study Guide (BWP000032)	$1.95	_____	_____
Genesis 12—50: Family Matters—Teaching Guide (BWP000035)	$2.45	_____	_____
Leviticus, Numbers, Deuteronomy—Study Guide (BWP000053)	$2.35	_____	_____
Leviticus, Numbers, Deuteronomy—Large Print Study Guide (BWP000052)	$2.35	_____	_____
Leviticus, Numbers, Deuteronomy—Teaching Guide (BWP000054)	$2.95	_____	_____
Joshua, Judges—Study Guide (BWP000047)	$2.35	_____	_____
Joshua, Judges—Large Print Study Guide (BWP000046)	$2.35	_____	_____
Joshua, Judges—Teaching Guide (BWP000048)	$2.95	_____	_____
1 and 2 Samuel—Study Guide (BWP000002)	$2.35	_____	_____
1 and 2 Samuel—Large Print Study Guide (BWP000001)	$2.35	_____	_____
1 and 2 Samuel—Teaching Guide (BWP000003)	$2.95	_____	_____
1 and 2 Kings: Leaders and Followers—Study Guide (BWP001025)	$2.95	_____	_____
1 and 2 Kings: Leaders and Followers Large Print Study Guide (BWP001026)	$3.15	_____	_____
1 and 2 Kings: Leaders and Followers Teaching Guide (BWP001027)	$3.45	_____	_____
Job, Ecclesiastes, Habakkuk, Lamentations: Dealing with Hard Times—Study Guide (BWP001016)	$2.75	_____	_____
Job, Ecclesiastes, Habakkuk, Lamentations: Dealing with Hard Times—Large Print Study Guide (BWP001017)	$2.85	_____	_____
Job, Ecclesiastes, Habakkuk, Lamentations: Dealing with Hard Times—Teaching Guide (BWP001018)	$3.25	_____	_____
Psalms and Proverbs: Songs and Sayings of Faith—Study Guide (BWP001000)	$2.75	_____	_____
Psalms and Proverbs: Songs and Sayings of Faith—Large Print Study Guide (BWP001001)	$2.85	_____	_____
Psalms and Proverbs: Songs and Sayings of Faith—Teaching Guide (BWP001002)	$3.25	_____	_____
Mark: Jesus' Works and Words—Study Guide (BWP001022)	$2.95	_____	_____
Mark: Jesus' Works and Words—Large Print Study Guide (BWP001023)	$3.15	_____	_____
Mark:Jesus' Works and Words—Teaching Guide (BWP001024)	$3.45	_____	_____
Jesus in the Gospel of Mark—Study Guide (BWP000066)	$1.95	_____	_____
Jesus in the Gospel of Mark—Large Print Study Guide (BWP000065)	$1.95	_____	_____
Jesus in the Gospel of Mark—Teaching Guide (BWP000067)	$2.45	_____	_____
Luke: Journeying to the Cross—Study Guide (BWP000057)	$2.35	_____	_____
Luke: Journeying to the Cross—Large Print Study Guide (BWP000056)	$2.35	_____	_____
Luke: Journeying to the Cross—Teaching Guide (BWP000058)	$2.95	_____	_____
The Gospel of John: The Word Became Flesh—Study Guide (BWP001008)	$2.75	_____	_____
The Gospel of John: The Word Became Flesh—Large Print Study Guide (BWP001009)	$2.85	_____	_____
The Gospel of John: The Word Became Flesh—Teaching Guide (BWP001010)	$3.25	_____	_____
Acts: Toward Being a Missional Church—Study Guide (BWP001013)	$2.75	_____	_____
Acts: Toward Being a Missional Church—Large Print Study Guide (BWP001014)	$2.85	_____	_____
Acts: Toward Being a Missional Church—Teaching Guide (BWP001015)	$3.25	_____	_____
Romans: What God Is Up To—Study Guide (BWP001019)	$2.95	_____	_____
Romans: What God Is Up To—Large Print Study Guide (BWP001020)	$3.15	_____	_____
Romans: What God Is Up To—Teaching Guide (BWP001021)	$3.45	_____	_____

2 Corinthians:Takng Ministry Personally—Study Guide (BWP000008)	$2.35	_____	_____
2 Corinthians:Takng Ministry Personally—Large Print Study Guide (BWP000007)	$2.35	_____	_____
2 Corinthians:Takng Ministry Personally—Teaching Guide (BWP000009)	$2.95	_____	_____
1, 2 Timothy, Titus, Philemon—Study Guide (BWP000092)	$2.75	_____	_____
1, 2 Timothy, Titus, Philemon—Large Print Study Guide (BWP000091)	$2.85	_____	_____
1, 2 Timothy, Titus, Philemon—Teaching Guide (BWP000093)	$3.25	_____	_____
Hebrews and James—Study Guide (BWP000037)	$1.95	_____	_____
Hebrews and James—Teaching Guide (BWP000038)	$2.45	_____	_____
Revelation—Study Guide (BWP000084)	$2.35	_____	_____
Revelation—Large Print Study Guide (BWP000083)	$2.35	_____	_____
Revelation—Teaching Guide (BWP000085)	$2.95	_____	_____

Coming for use beginning September 2008

Ephesians, Philippians, Colossians—Study Guide (BWP001060)	$3.25	_____	_____
Ephesians, Philippians, Colossians—Large Print Study Guide (BWP001061)	$3.55	_____	_____
Ephesians, Philippians, Colossians—Teaching Guide (BWP001062)	$3.75	_____	_____

Cost of items (Order value) _____

Shipping charges (see chart*) _____

TOTAL _____

Standard (UPS/Mail) Shipping Charges*	
Order Value	Shipping charge
$.01—$9.99	$6.00
$10.00—$19.99	$7.00
$20.00—$39.99	$8.00
$40.00—$79.99	$9.00
$80.00—$99.99	$12.00
$100.00—$129.99	$14.00
$130.00—$149.99	$18.00
$150.00—$199.99	$21.00
$200.00—$249.99	$26.00
$250.00 and up	10% of order value

*Plus, applicable taxes for individuals and other taxable entities (not churches) within Texas will be added. Please call 1-866-249-1799 if the exact amount is needed prior to ordering.

Please allow three weeks for standard delivery. For express shipping service: Call 1-866-249-1799 for information on additional charges.

YOUR NAME

PHONE

YOUR CHURCH

DATE ORDERED

MAILING ADDRESS

CITY

STATE   ZIP CODE

MAIL this form with your check for the total amount to
BAPTISTWAY PRESS, Baptist General Convention of Texas,
333 North Washington, Dallas, TX 75246-1798
(Make checks to "Baptist Executive Board.")

OR, **FAX** your order anytime to: 214-828-5376, and we will bill you.

OR, **CALL** your order toll-free: 1-866-249-1799
(M-Th 8:30 a.m.-8:30 p.m.; Fri 8:30 a.m.-5:00 p.m. central time),
and we will bill you.

OR, **E-MAIL** your order to our internet e-mail address:
baptistway@bgct.org, and we will bill you.

OR, **ORDER ONLINE** at www.baptistwaypress.org.

We look forward to receiving your order! Thank you!